Christianity Book for Women

CRAFTED BY SKRIUWER

Copyright © 2024 by Skriuwer.

All rights reserved. No part of this book may be used or reproduced in any form whatsoever without written permission except in the case of brief quotations in critical articles or reviews.

For more information, contact : **kontakt@skriuwer.com** (www.skriuwer.com)

TABLE OF CONTENTS

CHAPTER 1: INTRODUCTION TO FAITH IN JESUS

Understanding true belief in Jesus as the foundation of Christian living
Seeing how Jesus cared for women and showed them value
Discovering why faith matters in daily decisions
Building a life on God's unwavering truth

CHAPTER 2: THE POWER OF THE BIBLE

Recognizing Scripture as God's guiding Word
Learning how it brings wisdom and comfort
Exploring practical ways to study and apply biblical truths
Discovering God's character through His written revelation

CHAPTER 3: PRAYER & COMMUNICATION WITH GOD

Seeing prayer as daily, honest conversation with God
Overcoming barriers like doubt or busyness
Practicing practical steps to strengthen a prayer life
Learning to listen for God's guidance

CHAPTER 4: CARING FOR OTHERS WITH LOVE

Understanding the call to show kindness in everyday life
Showing compassion to family, friends, and strangers
Balancing service with healthy boundaries
Reflecting God's heart for people in practical ways

CHAPTER 5: WORK, GOALS, & GODLY PRINCIPLES

Viewing work as part of God's plan and blessing
Setting goals with wisdom and humility
Staying true to Christian values in the workplace
Managing time and resources under God's guidance

CHAPTER 6: FRIENDSHIPS AND SUPPORT

Building healthy relationships that encourage faith
Overcoming loneliness and forming genuine bonds
Handling conflicts with grace and understanding
Nurturing a supportive community around shared values

CHAPTER 7: INNER STRENGTH & GOOD HABITS

Developing daily routines that build character
Replacing harmful thoughts with biblical truths
Growing physically, mentally, and spiritually
Staying resilient in a demanding world

CHAPTER 8: RELATIONSHIPS AND HOLY LIVING

Honoring God through pure and respectful relationships
Practicing forgiveness and healthy communication
Understanding boundaries and commitment
Maintaining a Christ-centered focus in close bonds

CHAPTER 9: OVERCOMING WORRY AND FEAR

Identifying and challenging anxious thoughts
Turning worries into honest prayer
Learning how trust in God frees us from fear
Practicing daily steps to find inner peace

CHAPTER 10: STUDYING SCRIPTURE CAREFULLY

Diving deeper into God's Word with purpose
Using methods and tools for solid Bible study
Avoiding misconceptions and taking verses in context
Applying Scriptural truths to life's real questions

CHAPTER 11: GUIDING CHILDREN IN CHRISTIAN TEACHING

Teaching the next generation about Jesus
Modeling consistent faith at home
Using age-appropriate methods to share Bible truths
Balancing love and discipline under God's wisdom

CHAPTER 12: LOOKING TO CHRISTIAN LEADERS FOR HELP

Understanding the role of pastors, mentors, and counselors
Seeking wise counsel and spiritual guidance
Recognizing qualities of trustworthy leadership
Handling disappointments and staying anchored in God

CHAPTER 13: FACING HARD TIMES WITH STRENGTH

Understanding why difficulties occur in life
Learning to lean on God during crises
Finding comfort, hope, and growth through trials
Seeking community support and practical strategies

CHAPTER 14: FORGIVENESS AND MERCY

Letting go of hurt and resentment
Embracing God's model of mercy toward us
Practicing healthy boundaries alongside forgiveness
Experiencing freedom that comes from releasing bitterness

CHAPTER 15: BEING A GOOD EXAMPLE

Living with integrity and kindness day to day
Setting a tone of respect in family and work
Learning from mistakes and handling criticism with grace
Reflecting God's character in every interaction

CHAPTER 16: USING OUR GIFTS FOR GOD

Discovering talents and spiritual gifts
Overcoming obstacles like fear or comparison
Serving inside and outside the church community
Finding joy and purpose through active involvement

CHAPTER 17: TRUSTING GOD WITH OUR PLANS

Balancing personal goals with God's sovereignty
Turning anxiety about the future into trust
Handling delays, closed doors, and redirection
Finding peace in the knowledge that God guides each step

CHAPTER 18: HOLDING ON TO HOPE EACH DAY

Distinguishing genuine hope from wishful thinking
Staying positive despite discouraging news or events
Feeding hope through gratitude, Scripture, and prayer
Sharing hope with others who feel lost or uncertain

CHAPTER 19: WALKING WITH FAITH & CONFIDENCE

Building a secure identity in Christ
Overcoming setbacks, fear of failure, and comparison
Standing firm under pressure with peaceful boldness
Balancing humility and courage in everyday life

CHAPTER 20: FINAL THOUGHTS AND NEXT STEPS

Recapping core lessons learned throughout the book
Forming a personal plan for continued spiritual growth
Encouraging others and passing on what God has shown us
Moving forward with faith, hope, and love in Christ

CHAPTER 1: INTRODUCTION TO FAITH IN JESUS

Faith in Jesus is the foundation for Christian living. When we talk about having faith in Jesus, we mean putting our trust in who He is and what He has done. Many women today want a clear purpose and real peace. They look in different places, but deep peace comes from God. Faith in Jesus is the solid ground that can help us stand strong when life feels uncertain.

In this chapter, we will look at what it means to believe in Jesus, why that belief matters, and how it shapes our daily decisions. We will also see how Jesus treated women in the Bible, showing kindness, respect, and understanding. Through His example, we learn how to follow the path God wants for us. This chapter will give clear reasons to build your life on Jesus and show how His teachings can lead to a new way of living.

What Is Faith in Jesus?

Faith in Jesus means trusting that Jesus is the Son of God, trusting in His life, death, and resurrection. Faith is more than a feeling. It affects how we act and think. It also involves knowing that Jesus has the power to save us from our sins. Sins are the wrong things we do and the good things we fail to do. Faith in Jesus is not a guess or a random thought. It is a confident trust that He is real and that He has done what the Bible says He has done.

Some people think faith is just blind belief. But faith in Jesus is based on what the Bible teaches. We believe that He was a real person who walked on earth, taught people about God, died on a cross, and rose again. We also believe that He can forgive our sins and change our hearts. This trust is grounded in the reliable words of the Bible and in the witness of those who saw Him in person.

Why Is Faith Important?

Faith in Jesus is important because it connects us to God. In the Christian view, humans were made to have a relationship with God. But sin (the bad things in us and in the world) broke that relationship. Jesus died to fix this break, and faith in Him is how we accept that healing. Without faith, we cannot fully enter into God's plan for our lives. We would be cut off from the full sense of hope and purpose that only God can give.

Faith also helps us make sense of life. Many people ask questions about why bad things happen or why the world seems so broken. The Bible teaches us that sin has caused much of the trouble in the world. Jesus came to bring us back to God so that one day, all things will be made right. This plan might not unfold instantly, but we trust it will happen because God is faithful.

Jesus and Women

In the time of Jesus, women did not always have the same status as men in society. Yet, Jesus treated women with deep respect. We see this in several Bible stories. For example, there is a story about Jesus speaking with a woman at a well. Many people looked down on this woman. She had made bad choices, and she felt ashamed. But Jesus spoke kindly to her, asked her for water, and then offered her a new way to live by trusting in Him. This story shows that Jesus cares for women, listens to them, and welcomes them.

There are other times when Jesus reached out to women who were hurting. Whether they were sick or feeling hopeless, Jesus was kind to them. He showed that women matter to God and that they have a role in His kingdom. When we see how Jesus treated women, we learn how God values us. This is one reason why many women find comfort and confidence in Jesus. They see that He does not treat them as less important. Instead, He cares for them, teaches them, and gives them an important place in His plan.

How Faith Helps Us Find Purpose

One big question many people ask is, "What is my purpose in life?" For Christians, the main purpose is to know God and to follow Him. This might sound simple, but it shapes everything. If our purpose is to honor God, then our choices start to look different. We learn to care more about what God wants than about what the world says.

Women face many questions today: Should I focus on my career, or on my home, or both? How do I handle family and social life? How do I deal with pressure from the world? Faith in Jesus provides a framework that helps us with these decisions. It reminds us that God's way is the best way, even if other people do not understand it.

Our purpose as Christians is not only about ourselves. It is also about serving others and spreading the good news of Jesus. When we understand that God gave us gifts (such as skills, talents, and personalities), we can use those gifts in meaningful ways. We realize that each day can be an offering to God. This gives great meaning to our tasks, whether at home or in the workplace.

Common Misunderstandings About Faith

Some people think that once you decide to trust in Jesus, all your problems go away. That is not true. Christians still face trouble, sickness, and disappointment. The difference is that we now have the power of God with us. We have His wisdom and strength to guide us. Another misunderstanding is that faith must be perfect. In reality, people sometimes wrestle with doubt. The Bible shows us that God is patient with people who have questions. What matters is that we come to Him with a humble heart, trusting that He can guide us through uncertainty.

Faith also does not mean we stop thinking or asking questions. Instead, we use our minds to study God's Word and grow in understanding. We ask questions so we can learn more. Faith is not opposed to thinking. It includes a readiness to learn and grow. True faith keeps us curious about God's ways.

Making Faith Personal

It is one thing to read about faith, but it is another thing to live by it. How do we move from having an idea about Jesus to having a deep trust in Him? First, we must accept that we cannot save ourselves. No matter how hard we try, we fail in various ways. We might fail morally, or we might fail to live up to our own standards. We need a Savior.

Jesus is that Savior. We can pray to Him, asking Him to forgive us for our wrongdoings and to guide us. Then, we believe that He does forgive us, because that is what the Bible teaches. Once we have taken this step, we start to live each day by looking to Him for help. This does not mean we will be perfect right away, but it does mean we have a new direction. Our hearts will gradually change as we follow His teaching.

We can strengthen our faith by reading the Bible (we will talk about this more in the next chapter), praying regularly (covered later), and spending time with other Christians. When we are around people who share the same values, we can encourage each other. This helps our faith grow.

Faith and Daily Life

Faith in Jesus is not just about going to church on Sunday. It should change how we behave each day. This includes how we handle our responsibilities at home, at work, and with friends. If our faith is real, it will show in the love we show to others and in our honesty. We might start to see changes in how we talk, how we solve problems, and how we treat people.

For example, suppose you have a conflict with a friend. Before you had faith in Jesus, you might have tried to handle it on your own. But now, you might remember that Jesus said to love your neighbor and to forgive. You pray about the problem, seek guidance from the Bible, and try to resolve it in a way that pleases God. This is how faith touches day-to-day living.

Challenges and Opportunities for Women

Women have unique challenges in life, including certain health issues, social pressures, and cultural expectations. Faith in Jesus can be a source of comfort and direction. Women might also have special opportunities to serve God through their relationships with family, friends, and the community. Some women use their gifts in teaching, helping children learn about Jesus, or caring for those who are sick. Others might support church projects or show kindness in places like the workplace or in volunteer settings.

Faith in Jesus gives us a reason to be kind, to stand for what is right, and to stay strong even when things get tough. It helps us remain steady when people or society send confusing messages. Jesus sets the standard for right living, and that standard applies to men and women in different ways. We learn from Him how to live with humility and with strength.

The Role of Grace

We cannot talk about faith without talking about grace. Grace means favor we do not earn. Because of Jesus' sacrifice, we can find mercy and kindness from God even though we do not deserve it. This is good news for anyone who feels weighed down by past mistakes. We all fail at times. But God's grace covers those failures. It gives us a fresh start.

Grace is also a powerful force that changes us. It helps us realize that just as God forgives us, we should forgive others. This can be a life-changing concept, especially for women who might have felt overlooked or hurt. Once we understand that God loves us with an unearned love, we begin to see our worth in His eyes. That worth is not tied to looks, success, or the opinions of others. It is based on God's steady view of us as His children.

Faith and a New Way of Life

When we put our trust in Jesus, it leads to changes in our thoughts, words, and actions. This does not happen overnight. It is a daily process of choosing to follow Jesus rather than following selfish desires. These changes might show up in small decisions, such as how we spend our time, the words we use, and the people we choose to help.

Over time, this new way of life becomes more natural. We begin to care more about pleasing God than about pleasing ourselves. We might still struggle with temptations, but faith helps us fight them. When we fail, we can ask for forgiveness and keep moving forward. We are not stuck in our old way of living because Jesus makes all things new.

Looking at Role Models

It is often helpful to look at Christian women who have walked this path before us. We can see women in the Bible who showed faith in hard circumstances. For instance, Hannah was a woman in the Old Testament who longed for a child. She prayed to God earnestly, and He gave her a son. Hannah responded by dedicating her child to God's service. This story teaches us that God hears our prayers and that He might answer in unexpected ways.

In the New Testament, we read about Mary, the mother of Jesus. She was a young woman who was given a very big responsibility. She had questions, but she trusted God's plan. Through her life, we see the importance of humbly following God's call. We also see Mary Magdalene, who was a close follower of Jesus. She was the first person to see Jesus after He rose from the dead. Women in the Bible are often lifted up as examples of faith, kindness, and obedience. These stories can help us see what God can do in our own lives when we trust Him.

Practical Steps for Growing in Faith

1. **Read the Bible each day**: A short passage from the Gospels (Matthew, Mark, Luke, or John) is a great start. Let the words show you who Jesus is.
2. **Pray with honesty**: Tell God what is on your mind. Ask Him to teach you. You do not need fancy language. Simple words from the heart matter.
3. **Talk with believers**: Find at least one or two friends who share your faith. Discuss what you are learning, encourage each other, and help each other handle tough times.
4. **Seek out good teaching**: Look for a church that teaches the Bible in a clear way. If possible, find a small group or class where you can learn more and ask questions.
5. **Apply what you learn**: Faith is not just knowledge. It includes applying God's truth in daily decisions. Ask yourself, "How does what I read in the Bible affect my day?"

These steps might seem small, but they can bring big growth over time. By putting these things into practice, you will notice changes in your heart and attitude. You might find new peace and understanding as you rely on Jesus.

Obstacles to Growing in Faith

Many obstacles can pop up. One of them is too much busyness. If our schedules are packed, we might forget to pray or read the Bible. Another obstacle is doubt. We might wonder if God truly cares. In those moments, talking to a trusted friend or church leader can be helpful. Sometimes, a personal problem like anger, bitterness, or fear can also hold us back. We should bring these problems to God and, if needed, get help from wise counselors or mentors.

Some women worry that they are not good enough to have faith. They fear God might reject them because of their past. But the Bible shows us that Jesus came for people who have messed up. No matter what we have done, we can come to Jesus in faith. He receives those who turn to Him in sincere trust.

The Role of Service in Strengthening Faith

One of the surprising ways to grow in faith is to serve others. When we take our focus off ourselves and look at how we can help, we begin to learn about God's love in a fresh way. This might include volunteering at church, cooking a meal for someone who is sick, or offering help to a neighbor. Serving does not always have to be official. It can be simple acts of kindness. When we show kindness to others, our faith deepens because we start to see how God's love moves through us.

Serving also reminds us that God gave each person unique gifts to share. Some women are good at listening and comforting others. Some women have skills in planning and organizing. Others might be good at teaching children. Whatever your skills are, there is a place for them in God's plan. Using those skills in a helpful way can increase your faith.

Faith Brings Hope

A major benefit of faith is hope. Hope is the confident expectation that God's promises will come to pass. When we are weighed down by family problems, health issues, or worries about the future, hope tells us that God is still in control. This hope is not based on false optimism. It is based on the Bible's promises that God has a perfect plan and that He is stronger than any problem we face. Women who hold on to this hope can face challenges with calm hearts. They know their future rests in God's hands.

Strength in Weakness

Many women feel weak at times. We might feel physical weakness, emotional weakness, or social pressure. The Bible teaches that God's power is made perfect in our weakness. This means God can show His strength through our frailty. When we admit our need and ask for His help, He can do things that are beyond our own power. Faith in Jesus makes this possible, because Jesus opens the door for us to have a close relationship with God. No longer are we alone in our struggles.

This knowledge can give us courage to face even the hardest problems. We do not need to pretend we have everything together. We can be honest about our struggles. Through prayer and trust, we let God work in us. Over time, people might see how we handle tough moments and wonder how we do it. That is when we can point to Jesus, saying that He is the source of our strength.

Conclusion of Chapter 1

Faith in Jesus is not just an idea. It is a life-changing reality. Through faith, we find forgiveness, hope, and a new way to live. We also find that Jesus values women and welcomes them to be part of His plan. If you have ever felt unimportant or overlooked, know that Jesus sees you and cares for you. He wants to give you the peace and purpose that only He can provide.

This chapter opened the door to what it means to have faith in Jesus. We looked at why it matters and how it affects our daily life. Faith will be a central theme in all the chapters ahead. It ties into everything else: reading the Bible, praying, caring for others, building good habits, and handling life's problems. As we move forward, keep in mind that faith in Jesus is the root of all Christian growth. If you keep this focus, you will find the purpose and joy you are seeking.

CHAPTER 2: THE POWER OF THE BIBLE

The Bible is often called the Word of God. It is the main guide for Christians who want to learn about God's ways. Many women wonder how to make sense of life. The Bible provides wisdom for practical decisions and also answers deeper questions of the heart. In this chapter, we will look at why the Bible matters so much, how it came to us, and how we can read it in a way that helps us grow in faith and purpose.

Why the Bible Matters

The Bible is not just another book. It is made up of many books written over centuries by different writers. Yet, Christians believe it was all guided by the Holy Spirit. That means God worked through human writers to share His truth. The Bible tells the big story of how God created the world, how sin entered the world, and how God set a plan of salvation through Jesus. It also gives us rules for living, words of comfort, and hope for the future.

The Bible helps us understand who God is. We learn that God is loving, holy, just, and patient. We see His character through the stories and teachings. We also see our place in His plan. Without the Bible, we might guess what God is like, but we would not have a reliable record of His actions and words. With the Bible, we can know God in a clear way.

Different Parts of the Bible

The Bible has two main parts: the Old Testament and the New Testament. The Old Testament tells about creation, the early history of God's people, and the laws God gave them. It also has writings of prophets who pointed forward to Jesus. The New Testament tells about the life of Jesus, the growth of the early church, and teaching for believers.

Within these two parts, you will find different types of writing:

1. **Historical books**: These describe events that happened, such as in Genesis, Exodus, Joshua, and so on.

2. **Poetry and wisdom**: Books like Psalms and Proverbs provide songs, prayers, and wise sayings.
3. **Prophetic books**: Writers like Isaiah and Jeremiah spoke messages from God, warning people to turn back to Him.
4. **Gospels** (in the New Testament): Matthew, Mark, Luke, and John give four accounts of the life, death, and resurrection of Jesus.
5. **Letters**: Writers like Paul, Peter, and John wrote letters to churches, giving instruction and encouragement.
6. **Apocalyptic writing**: The book of Revelation describes future events in symbolic ways.

Knowing these kinds of writing helps us understand the Bible better. We realize that a poem in Psalms is different from a historical account in the Gospels. Both are true, but they convey truth in different styles.

How the Bible Guides Our Lives

The Bible does not just tell us what happened in the past; it also shows how God wants us to live today. For example, the Ten Commandments teach us basic moral guidelines: do not steal, do not lie, do not harm others, honor your father and mother, and so on. In the New Testament, Jesus sums up the law by saying we should love God with all we are and love our neighbors as ourselves.

These teachings shape our decisions at home, at work, and in the community. They teach us to live in a way that honors God and helps people around us. Many women find that when they follow these teachings, they have more peace and less chaos. God's rules are not meant to weigh us down. They protect us from harm and help us to thrive in His design.

Reading the Bible for Strength and Comfort

Sometimes life is hard, and we feel alone. The Bible gives many words of comfort. In Psalms, for example, we see honest prayers from people who felt afraid, sad, or confused. Yet, they turned to God and found He was faithful. When we read these passages, we can find strength for our own troubles. We realize that many believers before us have faced struggles and found hope in God.

If you are feeling worried, you might read passages that talk about God's care, like Psalm 23, which says God is our shepherd. If you feel guilty about something, you can read 1 John 1:9, which says if we confess our sins, God forgives us. These are just examples of how the Bible can speak to different areas of our lives. It tells us that no problem is too big or too small for God to handle.

How to Begin Reading

For some women, the Bible can feel overwhelming. It is a big book, and they might not know where to start. A good approach is to begin with one of the Gospels, such as John. This will give you a picture of who Jesus is and what He taught. You can read a little each day, maybe a chapter or a few verses, and then think about what you read.

Another idea is to pick a book like Psalms or Proverbs for daily encouragement or wisdom. Psalms is helpful when you feel emotional, whether happy or sad. Proverbs is filled with short sayings that give wise advice for everyday life. Some people also like to read from both the Old Testament and the New Testament each day, so they get a balanced view.

Making It a Habit

A big key to getting the most out of the Bible is reading it regularly. We can compare it to eating. Just as our bodies need daily food, our souls need daily spiritual nourishment. If we only read once a month, we might not grow as much. Setting aside a specific time each day, even if it is only a few minutes, can make a big difference.

Some women read in the morning before the day starts. Others read during lunch breaks or at night before bed. Find a time that works for you and stick to it. Over time, you might find yourself looking forward to this quiet time with God's Word.

Understanding What You Read

Sometimes, we might read the Bible and still feel confused. It helps to have a few tools. One tool is a good study Bible that has notes and references. These notes can explain background details. Another tool is a concordance or a simple online search that can point you to related verses.

You can also read with a friend or a study group. Discussing a passage can give fresh insights. Each person might see a different angle, and that can make the words come alive. The main goal is not just to gain facts but to understand how the words apply to life. Ask yourself questions like, "What does this teach me about God?" and "How should this change my behavior or attitude?"

The Bible and Modern Questions

Some people think the Bible is outdated. They say the world has changed and these old words do not apply. But Christians believe that the Bible's truths never change, even if society does. For example, the Bible teaches us to tell the truth. That was right in the past, and it is right now. The Bible also teaches about helping the poor and caring for children. These are timeless truths.

When we face new problems that are not spelled out in the Bible (such as issues with technology or complex relationships), we can look for guiding principles. The Bible teaches love, honesty, purity, and faithfulness. We can take these principles and apply them to modern challenges. Through prayer and careful thought, we can see how God's Word can guide us today.

How the Bible Points to Jesus

From the start of Genesis to the end of Revelation, the Bible points to Jesus. The Old Testament looks forward to a Savior who would rescue humanity from sin. The New Testament tells us that Jesus is that Savior. Even books that do not mention His name show our need for His saving work. This is what makes the Bible different from any other religious or historical text: it all focuses on Jesus and His role in God's plan.

When we read the Old Testament, we see patterns of sacrifice and promises of deliverance. These are fulfilled in Jesus when we get to the New Testament. For example, the Passover lamb in Exodus foreshadows how Jesus would be the final Lamb who takes away sin. These connections show that the Bible is one big story with Jesus at the center.

Common Struggles with the Bible

Many women find certain parts of the Bible hard to read, such as the long lists of names or laws in the Old Testament. They might feel discouraged and wonder why these are included. It helps to remember that every part of the Bible had meaning in its original context. Those names show us that God cares about families and individuals. Those laws show us what holiness looked like in ancient times. They also show how we need a better way to be right with God, which comes through Jesus.

Another struggle is making time. Life can be busy with family, work, and other duties. We might tell ourselves we will read later. But then the day slips away. One way to tackle this is to set a realistic goal. Maybe you aim to read for five minutes a day. That might not seem like much, but it is better than not reading at all. Once it becomes a habit, you might gradually increase your reading time.

Examples of the Bible's Power in People's Lives

The Bible has changed many lives in remarkable ways. There are stories of people who were depressed or hopeless, and after reading the Bible, they found hope. Some people were going down a destructive path, and the Bible's words stopped them. Others faced heartbreak, and the Scriptures gave them peace. The Bible has been used in prisons, hospitals, and all around the world to bring light in dark places.

In the early centuries, many people risked their lives to share the Bible. This was because they believed it had the power to save souls. Even today, in some places, people are not allowed to own or read the Bible freely. Yet, they do so in secret because they value its message more than their own safety. That shows us how powerful these words can be.

Women in the Bible and Their Lessons for Us

We can learn much from women in the Bible. In the Old Testament, we see Ruth, who showed great devotion to her family. Her story teaches us about faithfulness and the reward that comes from trusting God's plan. In the New Testament, we see Lydia, a businesswoman who supported the ministry of Paul and opened her home for believers. Her story reminds us that women can have strong faith and influence.

There are also warnings from women in the Bible who made bad choices. The story of Jezebel shows the harm that comes from pride and turning away from God. We can learn lessons by seeing both good and bad examples. The Bible does not sugarcoat human failings. It shows people as they are, reminding us that we all need God's help.

Practical Tips for Studying the Bible

1. **Choose a readable translation**: Some translations use old forms of English, which can be hard to follow. Pick a translation that is clear, but still faithful to the original text.
2. **Pray before you read**: Ask God to help you understand. A simple prayer can open your heart to what He wants you to see.
3. **Keep a notebook**: Write down verses that stand out, questions you have, or insights you gain.
4. **Try reading plans**: Many reading plans are available online. Some cover the entire Bible in a year, while others focus on certain topics.
5. **Share what you learn**: Talking about the Bible with a friend can help you remember the lessons and put them into practice.

The Bible and Transforming the Mind

The Bible does more than give us rules. It shapes our thinking. Romans 12:2 says we should be transformed by the renewal of our minds. This means that as we read the Bible, our thoughts align more with God's thoughts. We begin to see ourselves and others through His eyes. We realize that we are loved by God. We also see that we should treat others with kindness.

Women who fill their minds with the teachings of the Bible often report greater peace and clarity. They find that negative thoughts like envy, bitterness, or fear start to lose power. The Word of God replaces those thoughts with truth. This can take time, but it is worth the effort.

Handling Difficult Passages

There are sections of the Bible that might seem confusing. Some passages describe violence or events that feel harsh. It is important to understand the context. Sometimes, the Bible is just reporting what happened, not saying it was good. Other times, God was judging a situation that was evil, and it may seem harsh from our point of view. In these cases, seeking the help of a wise teacher or a study resource can be useful.

Remember, even if we do not fully grasp a passage at first, we can learn something from it. It might show us the seriousness of sin or the great lengths God goes to in order to protect His people. Over time, as we keep studying, we might see a bigger picture that we missed before.

Using the Bible for Guidance

When you face a decision, the Bible can be a guide. For instance, if you are unsure whether something is right or wrong, check if it lines up with God's commands. Look for teachings about honesty, purity, respect for others, and so forth. If you see that a choice goes against what God says, that is a sign to avoid it. If it agrees with His teachings, that is a sign you are on the right path.

Sometimes, the Bible will not give a direct answer, but it will offer principles. For example, if you are thinking about taking a new job, you might not see a specific verse. But you can look at passages about working hard, being fair, and putting God first. Then you can pray for wisdom. The Bible's overall message is a compass that can direct us if we let it shape our thoughts.

Spreading the Word

Once you discover the power of the Bible, you might want to share it with others. This does not require preaching on a stage. It can be as simple as telling a friend about a helpful verse you read. Or you might give someone a copy of the Bible. Some women like to host small gatherings where they read and discuss a short passage. The goal is not to force anything on others, but to let them see the value of these truths.

Conclusion of Chapter 2

The Bible is God's Word that teaches us who He is and how He wants us to live. It shows us our need for Jesus and helps us grow in faith. By reading it regularly, applying its truths, and seeking to understand it better, we allow God to guide us. When we face confusion or trials, the Bible can ground us. When we feel weak, it can strengthen us. It also inspires us by showing us the lives of faithful women and men.

For women who want real purpose, the Bible provides clear direction. It does not always promise an easy road, but it gives us wisdom for every part of life. As you move forward, let the Bible be your main source of truth. Combine what you read with prayer, fellowship, and a willing heart. You will find that God's Word has the power to light your path and deepen your faith.

CHAPTER 3: PRAYER AND COMMUNICATION WITH GOD

Prayer is one of the most important parts of a Christian's life. It is the way we talk to God, but it is also a way for us to open our hearts to Him. Some people think prayer is complicated. Others might think they need special words to speak to God. In truth, prayer can be as simple as talking to a friend who cares. In this chapter, we will look at why prayer is important, how to pray, and how to overcome common problems that keep us from praying. We will also learn that prayer is not only about speaking; it is also about listening. By paying attention to God's leading, we can grow closer to Him each day.

Why Prayer Is Important

1. **Connection with God**: One key reason for prayer is to keep our connection with God strong. When we pray, we acknowledge that we need Him. We may be used to handling everything ourselves, but prayer reminds us that God is the one in control. By taking time to pray, we show Him respect and trust.
2. **Growth in Faith**: Prayer can build our faith. When we ask for God's help and see that help come, even in small ways, our trust in Him grows. When we bring our fears and worries to Him, we learn that He can handle them better than we can.
3. **Peace of Mind**: The world can be stressful. We face tasks at home, challenges at work, family pressures, and more. Talking to God about these things can bring calm. We do not always get quick answers, but we can let go of our anxieties, knowing we have given them over to the One who loves us.
4. **Guidance**: Through prayer, we seek God's guidance for our decisions. We might be unsure which step to take in our career or how to solve a family issue. By praying, we ask God to direct our thoughts, which can help us avoid hasty decisions.
5. **Protection**: There are times when we need protection—spiritually, emotionally, or physically. Prayer is a way to ask God for safety.

That does not mean bad things will never happen, but it does mean we trust God to watch over us, even in hard moments.

Types of Prayer

1. **Praise**: This is when we honor God for who He is. We think about His power, His goodness, and His patience. By focusing on these qualities, we remind ourselves that God is above all and worthy of our praise.
2. **Thanksgiving**: This involves saying thanks for what God has done. Many times we forget the good things in our lives. Saying thanks helps us remember that every good gift comes from God. It also keeps us from taking blessings for granted.
3. **Confession**: This type of prayer is about admitting our wrongdoings and asking for forgiveness. We all fall short in words, actions, or thoughts. Confession allows us to be honest with God. It also clears the guilt that sometimes weighs us down.
4. **Requests**: We often think of prayer as asking for help. That is indeed part of prayer. We can come to God with any need, big or small. We can ask for healing, wisdom, or even daily needs like food and shelter. God wants us to bring our concerns to Him.
5. **Listening**: This part can be overlooked. Prayer is not only about speaking; it is also about allowing God to speak to us. We might not hear an audible voice, but God can guide us through the Bible, through thoughts He places on our hearts, or through the counsel of wise friends.

How to Pray in a Simple Manner

Some people worry that they need long, fancy prayers. God does not require that. Here are some simple steps:

1. **Find a Quiet Place**: It helps to have a space free from distractions. This could be a corner in your home, your car during a break, or even a walk outside. The important thing is to have a calm environment.

2. **Speak Honestly**: Talk to God as you would talk to someone who truly cares. You do not have to use special words. Just express what you feel. If you are sad, tell Him. If you are grateful, tell Him. If you are confused, tell Him.
3. **Use the Bible**: You can read a passage from the Bible and then pray about what you read. This helps you focus on God's truth. For example, if you read a verse about God's care, you can thank Him for caring and then ask Him to help you trust Him more.
4. **Pause and Listen**: After you speak, take a moment to be still. This might feel odd at first, but it gives you a chance to reflect on what you have said and to sense any thought or nudge God places on your heart. You might recall a verse that applies to your situation.
5. **Keep It Up**: Prayer is like talking to a close friend daily rather than once a month. The more you do it, the more natural it feels. If you miss a day, do not give up. Simply begin again.

Barriers to Prayer

1. **Distractions**: We live in a busy world filled with alerts on our phones and tasks that never end. It is easy to forget prayer in the rush of daily life. One way to overcome this is to set a specific time to pray. Mark it on a calendar if needed.
2. **Doubt**: Sometimes people stop praying because they doubt God is listening. They might ask, "Why pray if God knows everything already?" But we pray because God wants a relationship with us. Also, by praying, we are shaped in the process. Even if the answer is not what we expect, prayer changes our perspective.
3. **Guilt or Shame**: Some women feel they are not worthy to pray because of past mistakes. But the Bible says God welcomes us. We can confess our wrongdoings to Him. He forgives and helps us move forward.
4. **Lack of Time**: Busy schedules can swallow our prayer time. One solution is to start small. Pray for two minutes when you wake up or before you go to sleep. You can also pray while doing routine tasks like washing dishes or driving to work.
5. **Discouragement**: If we do not see fast answers, we might feel discouraged. The Bible shows that answers can come slowly. We

keep praying, trusting that God is good and that His timing is better than ours.

Listening to God's Leading

Prayer is not just a list of requests. It is also a time to sense God's direction. How do we know we are hearing from God?

1. **Check with the Bible**: God will never ask you to do something that goes against what the Bible teaches. If you feel led to do something that clearly breaks His commands, that is not from Him.
2. **Consider Wise Counsel**: Talk to a trusted Christian friend or leader if you are unsure. They may help confirm if a thought lines up with God's truth.
3. **Look at Circumstances**: Sometimes doors open or close in ways that guide you. If you have been praying for direction and a specific opportunity appears, this might be God's leading. Pray more to confirm.
4. **Peace in Your Heart**: While feelings can be tricky, there is a certain calm that can come when you are following God's direction. If you sense that calm after seeking God in prayer, it could be a sign you are on the right track.

Group Prayer vs. Private Prayer

Both private and group prayer are important.

- **Private Prayer**: This is your personal time with God. It allows you to be completely honest without worrying about what others think. Private prayer helps you develop a deeper closeness with God.
- **Group Prayer**: Praying with friends or a church group can bring encouragement. You realize you are not alone in your struggles. You can support one another. Group prayer also teaches us to care about the needs of others, not just our own.

Learning from Jesus' Example

Jesus gave us an example of prayer. In the Gospels, we see Him waking up early to pray alone. He also prayed before big events, such as choosing His disciples. On the night before He died, He prayed intensely in a garden, asking for God's will to be done. From Jesus, we learn that prayer requires honesty, humility, and a willingness to follow God's plan. When His followers asked how to pray, He taught them what is often called the Lord's Prayer. It begins with honoring God's name and includes asking for daily needs, forgiveness, and deliverance from evil.

Practical Tips for a Steady Prayer Life

1. **Set Goals**: You might decide to pray for a few minutes each morning or evening. Having a goal can help you stay committed.
2. **Use a Prayer List**: Write down the names of people you want to pray for, issues in your own life, or things happening in the world. This keeps you organized so you do not forget.
3. **Try Different Postures**: Some people kneel, some sit, some stand. You can also pray while walking. The posture is not the focus, but sometimes changing how you position yourself can help you concentrate.
4. **Pray Scripture**: When you read a verse, turn it into a prayer. For example, if you read about God's kindness, you can pray, "God, thank You for being kind. Help me show kindness to others today."
5. **Stay Flexible**: Life can be unpredictable. If you cannot stick to your usual time, pray at a different time. The key is to maintain that connection with God.

Handling Unanswered Prayers

A challenging part of prayer is when it seems God is silent. There could be many reasons for this:

- **Timing**: Maybe God's answer is "wait." Our timeframe is often short, but God's view is bigger.
- **Different Answer**: Sometimes God answers in a way we did not expect. We might pray for a specific outcome, but God, in His wisdom, might give us something else that turns out to be better.
- **Testing of Faith**: Waiting can teach us patience and trust. It shows whether we only seek God for quick fixes or truly trust Him.

Even if you feel your prayers are unanswered, keep praying. You might later see that God was working in the background the entire time.

Testimonies of Changed Lives

Many stories exist of how prayer changed lives. For example, a woman might have prayed for a troubled marriage. Over time, she may have seen her husband's heart soften, or she might have found a new strength to handle her relationship. Another person might have prayed for healing from illness, and through the process, gained peace, even if the healing took a while. These accounts do not mean we always get exactly what we want, but they do show that God listens. They also remind us that prayer can bring change within us, making us more patient, wise, and reliant on God.

The Role of the Holy Spirit

The Bible teaches that the Holy Spirit helps us pray. Sometimes we do not even know what to say. The Holy Spirit can guide our hearts and express needs that go beyond words. He also comforts us and reminds us of what Jesus taught. When we sense a strong urge to pray for someone at a random time, it might be the Holy Spirit prompting us. Paying attention to this can lead to powerful moments of caring for others in prayer.

Using Written Prayers

Some people find help in written prayers, like those in a prayer book or the Psalms in the Bible. Reading these can guide your thoughts. They can help you find words when you are upset, lonely, or unsure what to say. However, be careful not to rely so heavily on written prayers that your communication with God becomes routine. God wants to hear your own thoughts, even if they are simple.

Praying for Others

Christians are called to pray for the needs of others, including friends, family, leaders, and even those who hurt us. When we pray for someone, it can change our attitude toward them. It can deepen our care for them. Sometimes we might want to hold anger against a person. But when we pray for them, we see them more as God sees them. This can bring healing and reduce our bitterness.

Praying for others also reminds us that the world is bigger than our personal worries. We might pray for people in other countries facing serious problems. We might not be able to solve those problems ourselves, but we can ask God to bring relief. This act of praying helps us stay aware of the needs around us.

Balancing Words and Action

Prayer should not replace action when action is needed. If we pray for the poor but never help them, something is missing. True prayer often leads us to do something practical. We ask God to provide for someone in need, and then we might sense that God wants us to be part of the answer. So we give or serve in a practical way. Prayer and action go hand in hand.

Prayer as a Lifelong Practice

Prayer is not something we master in a day. It is a lifelong practice. As we go through different phases of life, our prayers may change. A single woman might focus her prayers on her daily routines, her job, and her hopes for the future. A mother might pray for her children's well-being and growth. A retired woman might spend more time praying for others or for missionaries around the world. Each season of life can bring new focus to our prayers.

Finding Encouragement When Prayer Feels Dry

There might be times when prayer feels dull. You might not sense the closeness of God as before. This can happen for many reasons. It is important not to give up. Keep talking to God, even if you do not feel a strong response. Consider reading different parts of the Bible, or finding a friend you can pray with. Sometimes, a new approach or a fresh environment can help. Also, make sure to examine your life to see if there is any sin or unhealthy habit that might be blocking your closeness with God. If so, confess it and ask God to renew your heart.

Trusting God in All Circumstances

One of the greatest benefits of prayer is learning to trust God no matter what. We might face very hard situations: illness, financial problems, or broken relationships. Through prayer, we remind ourselves that God sees and cares. We still do what we can, but we understand our limitations. Knowing God is sovereign brings comfort. If we only prayed in good times, we would miss the deep closeness that can develop when we cry out to God in sadness or confusion. Over time, this trust can become unshakable, built on God's faithfulness.

Conclusion of Chapter 3

Prayer is a life-changing gift from God. It is how we bring our praise, thanks, confessions, and requests to Him. It is also how we hear His direction. We do not need to speak in a formal style. Simple, honest words from the heart are enough. Though distractions, doubts, and guilt can block our prayers, we can overcome them by setting aside time, trusting God's promises, and staying consistent.

As you put prayer into practice, you will see your faith deepen. You will learn to depend on God and notice His work in your life more often. You might also be inspired to pray for others, which can help you grow in compassion. Keep in mind that unanswered prayers do not mean God is absent. Instead, He might be teaching you patience, guiding you to a better path, or showing you that He has bigger plans.

Prayer is not complicated, but it does require commitment. As you continue to grow in faith, let prayer be the steady line of communication that keeps you close to God. In good times or bad, prayer stands as a lifeline to the One who made you and loves you. By holding onto that line, you will gain peace, wisdom, and the confidence that God is truly with you every step of the way.

CHAPTER 4: CARING FOR OTHERS WITH LOVE

In the Christian life, caring for others is not just a suggestion—it is a core teaching. Jesus told His followers to love their neighbors. He even said to care about enemies. This kind of attitude sets Christianity apart, because it calls us to do good to all people, not just those who treat us well. In this chapter, we will explore how women can show real kindness and concern in their homes, at church, in the workplace, and in the broader community. We will also consider some of the challenges that can arise when we try to help and how to handle them with wisdom.

Why Caring for Others Matters

1. **It Reflects God's Character**: God shows love to us in many ways, including forgiveness and blessings. When we care for others, we reflect a small part of that divine kindness. People see God's heart through our actions.
2. **It Strengthens Relationships**: Being thoughtful toward others can build deeper friendships, stronger family bonds, and healthier communities. When people see they are not alone in their struggles, they often feel more hopeful.
3. **It Fulfills a Command**: The Bible repeatedly instructs us to look out for the needs of others. Jesus highlighted love as the greatest command, next to loving God. Ignoring this call can lead to a self-centered life that lacks real purpose.
4. **It Brings Joy**: Helping others can bring a sense of contentment. Even small acts of kindness can brighten your day as well as someone else's.

Areas Where We Can Show Concern

1. **At Home**: This might be the first place we think of. We can cook meals for family members, listen when they have had a tough day,

or keep a peaceful environment. If there is conflict, showing kindness might involve offering forgiveness or stepping in with a helpful solution.
2. **In Friendships**: Good friends stand by each other through ups and downs. Caring for friends means being available when they need someone to talk to. It also means speaking truth when they might be making unwise choices, but doing so in a kind way.
3. **At Church**: Churches should be places where people can find help and support. You might help by volunteering in the children's class, preparing coffee and snacks, or visiting a church member who is sick or shut in. Even greeting new visitors warmly can make a difference.
4. **In the Community**: Our care should go beyond those closest to us. It might mean helping at a local shelter, donating food, or simply being a respectful neighbor. Sometimes it is just noticing the person next door who lives alone and might need a listening ear.
5. **In the Workplace**: If you work outside the home, you can show care by helping a coworker meet a deadline, offering to bring coffee for someone who is overwhelmed, or sharing an encouraging word. This does not mean pushing your faith on others in an unwelcome way. It simply means being thoughtful in your day-to-day interactions.

Practical Ways to Show Kindness

1. **Offer Support**: If someone is sick or has just had a baby, you could drop off a meal or watch their children for a bit. These practical helps can show God's love in tangible ways.
2. **Give a Listening Ear**: In a world full of noise, truly listening to someone can be a rare gift. Put your phone aside, give eye contact, and let them know you hear them.
3. **Speak Encouragement**: Words have the power to lift or discourage. Choose uplifting words. Let people know you believe in them. Remind them of God's faithfulness. A simple phrase like, "I'm here for you," can mean a lot.
4. **Pray for Others**: When you find out about someone's struggle, you can pray for them right then. If they are open to it, you can even

pray with them. This can be a powerful source of comfort, letting them know you truly care.
5. **Share Resources**: If you know about a helpful service or a way to solve a problem, pass that information along. Whether it is a job opening, a good book, or a support group, sharing can open doors for others.

Challenges in Caring for Others

Caring for others can be rewarding, but it also brings challenges:

1. **Time Constraints**: We all have busy schedules. We might feel we do not have enough hours in the day to take on someone else's needs. However, even small gestures can help. A text message or a short visit can still show support.
2. **Emotional Stress**: Helping others might mean hearing difficult stories or seeing painful situations. We might get overwhelmed if we try to carry their burdens alone. That is why we must remember that only God can handle everything. We do our part and trust Him for the rest.
3. **Burnout**: Some women try to do too much. They say yes to every request and end up exhausted. We need balance. It is not selfish to rest or to say no when our plate is too full. God wants us to serve with a cheerful heart, not out of guilt.
4. **Misunderstandings**: Sometimes our efforts to help might be taken the wrong way. People might think we are meddling or prideful. That is why it is important to show respect and ask before we step in. "Is there a way I can help?" is often better than just assuming.
5. **Personal Boundaries**: Caring for others does not mean letting people hurt us or take advantage of us. We can be kind and still keep healthy limits. If someone is abusing our kindness, it might be wise to seek advice from a counselor or pastor.

Learning from Jesus' Actions

Jesus showed us what true kindness looks like. He healed the sick, fed the hungry, and spent time with those society rejected. In one story, He stopped to help a woman who had been bleeding for many years. While many people passed her by, He called her "daughter" and restored her health. This shows how Jesus treated people as individuals. He was willing to give time, attention, and compassion. By looking at His actions, we see the standard for loving others. It is a standard that goes beyond words. It involves seeing a person's need and responding with a caring heart.

Letting Love Start in Our Hearts

Real care does not begin with our hands; it begins with our hearts. If we only try to do good deeds without genuine love inside, people can sense the difference. The Bible says that if we do great acts but do not have love, our actions mean little. So how do we grow a loving heart? We stay connected to God. We remember how He forgives us. We let gratitude for His kindness fill our hearts. That gratitude spills over into how we treat others. Each day, we can ask God to help us see people as He sees them.

Serving Without Looking for Praise

One temptation is to want attention or applause for doing good. Maybe we want people to know we donated money or gave time. Yet Jesus taught that doing acts of love in secret can be even more special, because we are not trying to impress others. God sees our heart. When we help someone without seeking credit, it shows humble service. This kind of selfless action can make a huge impact, because it points people's eyes to God, not to us.

Caring for Those Who Seem Difficult

It is easy to show kindness to people who treat us well. But Jesus challenges us to do good even to those who might be hard to like. This can include rude coworkers, neighbors with different views, or even people who have hurt us. Why do this? Because when we extend kindness in these situations, we show a higher standard of love. We also break the chain of anger or resentment. This does not mean we ignore harmful behavior, but we do not return hate for hate. Instead, we can do good and leave the final outcome to God.

Balancing Family Obligations

Many women feel torn between caring for their own families and caring for people outside their household. Family responsibilities are important. The Bible teaches us to look after our household. However, sometimes we can invite our family to help with acts of kindness. For example, if you plan to make a meal for a sick neighbor, ask your children or spouse to help with the cooking. That way, you do not neglect family time, and you teach them about serving others.

Encouraging Other Women

Women can face unique pressures—raising children, managing a home, dealing with body image issues, or balancing work and personal life. We can support each other by sharing honest stories, giving practical advice, and praying for each other. This kind of support group can be found at church or among Christian friends. We can also reach out to women who seem isolated. A phone call, a kind note, or an invite to coffee can remind someone that they are valued.

Using Our Gifts to Help Others

We all have different talents. One woman might be good at cooking, another at teaching, another at organizing events. Some have creative minds, while others are skilled at listening. Whatever your gifts are, you can use them to help others. Ask yourself, "What am I good at, and how can that bless someone today?" This question can open up many possibilities. Maybe you can tutor a child, sew blankets for a shelter, or fix someone's computer. No matter how small it seems, it can meet a need.

Avoiding Pride and Comparison

When we talk about caring for others, we should be cautious not to compare ourselves with other women. One person might be able to volunteer 10 hours a week, while another can only give 1 hour. One might have the finances to donate money, while another does not. We are not in a race to see who can do the most. God sees the heart behind the action. A small deed done with sincere love can have as much value as a bigger deed done without the right motive.

Also, we must guard against pride. If we start to think we are better than others because we help a lot, we lose humility. The Bible warns us to stay humble, remembering that all our talents and resources come from God.

Dealing with Disappointments

Sometimes we try to help someone, and they do not respond the way we hope. They might reject our help or fail to appreciate it. This can hurt our feelings. But God calls us to remain kind. We do not show kindness only to receive thanks. We do it because God has been kind to us. If we feel deeply hurt, we can pray and ask for healing. We can also talk with a trusted friend or pastor for advice. However, we should not let one bad experience stop us from helping others in the future.

Caring in Times of Crisis

During emergencies or disasters, the need for help becomes more urgent. This might be a medical crisis in a friend's life or a natural disaster affecting many people. We can pray for them, but we can also check if there is a practical way to assist. It could be as simple as giving someone a ride to the doctor or offering a spare room to a displaced family. These urgent moments can be opportunities to show genuine love. People often remember who stood by them when times were hardest.

Long-Term Support

Some needs are not fixed quickly. For example, if someone has a long-term illness or faces deep financial struggles, caring for them might require ongoing help. That can be tiring. We may need to organize a rotation with a few friends or church members so that one person is not overwhelmed. Long-term support also includes emotional support. Someone facing depression or grief might need ongoing conversation and prayer. These situations remind us that caring can be a marathon, not a quick sprint. We rely on God to give us strength and wisdom for the long haul.

Encouraging Others to Help

One person cannot handle every need in a community. This is why it is important to encourage others to be involved. You can share the story of a family in need with your Bible study group or your friends. Offer ideas on how to help. Sometimes people are willing to assist but do not know where to start. By pointing them in the right direction, you multiply the impact.

Keeping the Right Balance

While caring for others is good, we also need time to rest and take care of our own well-being. It is hard to pour into others if our own tank is empty. Jesus Himself took time to rest. After being with crowds, He would go to a quiet place to pray. This was not selfish; it was wise. If you find yourself constantly tired, you might need to step back for a short period. Ask someone else to step in. Then, after you recharge, you can return to serving with new energy.

Stories of Caring in Action

Throughout history, many Christian women have done remarkable works of kindness. Some started orphanages, others opened their homes to those in need, and many taught children who had no access to schools. Though you may not be called to open an orphanage, you can still make a difference. Even a small act can have a ripple effect. If you help one person, they might go on to help someone else. This chain of kindness can reach farther than you think.

Conclusion of Chapter 4

Caring for others is central to the Christian life. It shows the heart of God in ways that words alone cannot. When we show kindness at home, among friends, in church, at work, and in our neighborhoods, we let the light of Christ shine. Challenges will arise—time constraints, burnout, misunderstandings—but God can guide us through these if we ask Him. By studying the example of Jesus, we learn to see each person as valuable.

Remember, care starts with a heart changed by God's kindness. From there, it flows out in practical ways: a meal, a listening ear, a kind word, or a humble act of service. We do not do it for praise. We do it to reflect the love that God first showed us. As you step out to help others, you will not only bless them, but you will also find your own faith strengthened and your own life enriched.

In the next chapters, we will continue to explore how to live with real purpose in Christ. We will look at work, goals, relationships, and even the ways we handle fear. Keep in mind that our faith in Jesus, our grounding in the Bible, our practice of prayer, and our care for others are all pieces of a well-built Christian life. By growing in these areas, we grow closer to God and find deeper joy.

CHAPTER 5: WORK, GOALS, AND GODLY PRINCIPLES

Work is part of life. We might be employed in an office, run a small business, handle a busy household, or help in a volunteer setting. Some women do paid jobs, while others focus on raising children or caring for family members. Any way we look at it, work matters. It helps us meet needs, use our skills, and contribute to the good of others. In this chapter, we will talk about the purpose of work, how to set wise goals, and how to honor God through our efforts. We will also look at how to handle stress and keep our priorities in order.

Work as a Blessing

Some people see work as a burden, but the Bible shows that God gave work to humans from the beginning. In the book of Genesis, we see the first man tasked with caring for the garden. This was before wrongdoing entered the world, which means work was originally good. Later, sin brought hardship into work, but the idea of working itself was not a punishment.

When we work, we reflect a part of God's nature. He is a creator and sustainer of life. By working, we mirror that creative spark in small ways. We also learn discipline, patience, and how to solve problems. These can shape our hearts for the better. However, we must remember that our identity is not in our job title. Our identity is in being children of God. This means that whether we have a high-paying job, stay at home, or are between jobs, our worth stays the same in God's eyes.

Different Kinds of Work

1. **Employment Outside the Home**: Some women hold jobs in offices, schools, shops, or factories. Others run their own businesses. These roles can help support a family financially. They can also be ways to

share Christian values in the workplace through honesty, kindness, and respect.
2. **Work at Home**: Managing a household, raising children, or caring for older relatives is real work. It requires strong organization, patience, and emotional energy. Though it may not bring a paycheck, it builds healthy families and communities.
3. **Volunteer Work**: Helping at church, in the community, or with a charity can also be called work. Even if there is no pay, there is effort and time involved. Volunteer roles can be powerful ways to show care and to serve God.
4. **Seasonal and Part-Time Roles**: Many women take short-term or flexible positions that fit around family duties. They might do online jobs, tutoring, or help in local shops. These roles can still be ways to honor God if done with integrity.

No matter which path we are on, the Bible reminds us to do our work with a sincere heart. Colossians 3:23 says to work as if we are serving the Lord, not just people. This teaching lifts our eyes above the daily grind and shows that our work can have deeper meaning if done in the right spirit.

Setting Goals with Wisdom

Goals can give us direction. A goal might be a project at work, a plan to learn a new skill, or something at home like organizing a cluttered space. Setting goals helps us focus our time and energy. But as Christians, we should set them with wisdom.

1. **Seek God First**: Before making big decisions, pray and ask for God's guidance. The Bible says that when we trust the Lord and do not just depend on our own understanding, He will direct our path. This does not mean we wait for a voice from the sky. Instead, we combine prayer, reading Scripture, and sometimes talking to wise friends.
2. **Check Motives**: Ask yourself, "Why do I want this goal?" If the answer is to gain praise or to show off, it might not be the best motive. If the answer is to serve others, provide for your family, or use your gifts, then it can be a wise path.

3. **Be Realistic**: Goals should stretch us but should also be reachable. Setting a goal that is far outside our ability can lead to discouragement. For example, if you have never run before, aiming to run a marathon next week would be unwise. A better plan might be to start a regular exercise routine and slowly increase your distance.
4. **Plan Step by Step**: Break big goals into smaller steps. For instance, if you plan to learn a new language, set a goal to study for 15 minutes a day. Then, after a month, review your progress. Smaller steps help you stay motivated because you see gradual improvement.
5. **Stay Flexible**: Sometimes life changes and our goals need adjusting. Children get sick, unexpected bills come, or job conditions shift. We should hold our goals loosely, letting God redirect us when necessary.

Balancing Work and Rest

Some people think that to succeed, they must work non-stop. Yet, the Bible teaches the need for rest. In the Old Testament, there was a command to set aside one day each week to rest from regular work. While modern schedules can be demanding, the principle still applies. We all need time to recharge physically, mentally, and spiritually.

If we push ourselves too hard, we risk burnout. We might also neglect important relationships. Achieving a big career goal but losing family closeness is not real success. Neither is burning out our bodies until we are too exhausted to be kind or patient. By scheduling rest, we show that we trust God. We believe He can care for our needs, so we do not have to run ourselves into the ground.

Handling Stress and Pressure

Work can bring stress. Deadlines, difficult bosses, financial worries, or unending tasks at home can pile up. As Christians, we want to handle stress in a healthy way that honors God.

1. **Pray About Your Concerns**: Instead of letting your thoughts spin, take them to God. Say what is on your mind. Ask for help, wisdom, or an open door to solve your problem. This does not remove the stress instantly, but it gives you a place to put your worries.
2. **Organize and Prioritize**: Stress sometimes grows when tasks pile up without order. Make a list of what must be done first, second, and so on. If a task can wait, let it wait. If there is something someone else can do, ask for help. You do not have to do everything alone.
3. **Seek Wise Counsel**: If you feel stuck in a tough work situation, talk to someone you trust. This could be a mentor, a friend from church, or a professional counselor if the problems are serious. Sometimes a fresh perspective can point out steps forward that you did not see.
4. **Practice Self-Care**: Eat well, get enough sleep, and include activities that refresh your mind. For some, this could be a simple walk outdoors. For others, it might be reading a good book. Taking care of yourself is not selfish. It prepares you to do your work better.
5. **Remember Your Value**: Stress often comes from thinking our worth depends on success. But your true value is in being loved by God. When you grasp this, you can work hard without letting the results define your sense of self.

Doing Work That Honors God

No matter where you are employed or how you serve, you can reflect God's character:

1. **Honesty**: Avoid cutting corners or lying about performance. Be straightforward with clients, bosses, or co-workers. Integrity might cost you in some workplaces, but it brings lasting respect.
2. **Kindness**: Treat people as human beings, not obstacles. If a co-worker is having a bad day, ask if they need help. Speak politely, even when stressed. Small acts of kindness can stand out in a tense environment.

3. **Quality**: Offer your best effort. This does not mean perfection, but it does mean caring about the details and doing tasks to the best of your ability. Over time, people will see you as someone who can be trusted with responsibility.
4. **Fairness**: If you manage people or resources, do so fairly. Do not show bias. Pay what is due if you hire someone. Treat all people with respect, regardless of their position or background.
5. **Willingness to Learn**: Work can be a place where we grow in patience and skill. If we face criticism, we can learn from it rather than getting angry. If new methods appear, we can be open to them. Learning can be a way we show humility.

Money Matters

Work often ties to money. The Bible does not say money is evil, but it warns us about loving money too much. If our main drive is to get rich, we can fall into traps like greed or dishonesty. Instead, the Bible shows that money is a tool to be used wisely. It can meet our needs and help others.

1. **Saving**: It can be wise to save part of our income for the future or for emergencies. This does not mean living in fear of what might happen, but it shows good planning.
2. **Giving**: Sharing with others is a principle we see in Scripture. We do not give just when we have extra. We make it part of our budget to give to church or those in need. This develops a heart that trusts God more than our bank account.
3. **Spending Wisely**: Many families struggle with debt or overspending. Setting a budget can help us see where our money is going. It also helps us make sure we are not wasting resources on things that do not matter.
4. **Helping Family**: Part of our money might be used to support aging parents, children's education, or other family needs. We do our best within our means, trusting that God will supply as we handle finances carefully.

By keeping money in the right place, we avoid making it an idol. Instead, we use it to do good, care for loved ones, and live responsibly.

When Work Feels Unfulfilling

Many women go through seasons where their tasks feel boring or pointless. This can happen in a job that lacks excitement, or at home when chores pile up day after day. In these times, we can recall that our work is bigger than the task itself. It is an opportunity to develop character and serve God. Even a job we do not love can be a place where we learn patience, shape our attitude, and shine a light of hope to co-workers.

If a job is truly toxic or goes against our values, we can pray and look for a better position. Sometimes God leads us to stay a while longer to be a help or to learn something. Other times, He opens a door for us to move on. Each situation calls for prayer, wise counsel, and careful thinking. If we do have to remain, looking for small ways to make a difference can help us press on.

Setting Limits and Guarding Our Priorities

A busy job or a large set of duties at home can eat up all our time if we are not careful. This can hurt our relationships with God, family, and friends. Setting limits helps us keep a healthy balance. For example, you can decide not to check work emails after a certain hour. Or you can choose a certain day of the week to spend with family. These small steps keep work in its proper place.

We might also need to learn to say no to extra requests at times. This can be hard if we fear letting people down. But if we overextend, we might burn out or neglect our own family. God does not call us to meet every need that arises. He calls us to be faithful in what He has given us. By seeking God's wisdom, we can figure out where to invest our energy.

Examples of Women in the Bible Who Worked

1. **Ruth**: In the Old Testament, Ruth worked hard gleaning leftover grain in the fields to provide for herself and her mother-in-law. She showed dedication and kindness, and her story ends with blessing. Her diligence caught the attention of a man named Boaz, who respected her.
2. **Lydia**: In the New Testament, Lydia was a merchant who sold purple cloth. She was a businesswoman who became a believer in Jesus. She opened her home to traveling teachers and played a part in supporting the early church. Her story shows that business can be a way to honor God.
3. **Proverbs 31 Woman**: This passage describes a woman who manages many tasks. She buys fields, plants vineyards, and makes goods to sell. She looks after her household and helps the needy. Although it paints a high standard, it reminds us that women can be strong, resourceful, and godly in their work.

These examples show that women's work can be varied. Some are in farming, others in trade, and still others in household management. The common thread is a heart turned toward God and a willingness to serve faithfully.

Staying True to Your Values

In some workplaces, you might face pressure to act against your conscience. Maybe a boss wants you to lie on a report or treat customers unfairly. Perhaps co-workers encourage gossip or unethical shortcuts. As Christians, we are called to follow God's ways, even if it means facing disagreement or losing a job. This is not easy, but God can strengthen us to stand for what is right. Over time, we might gain respect for our integrity, or we might have to move on. In either case, we keep our conscience clear before God.

Helping Others with Their Goals

It is not just about our own work and goals. We can also help others with theirs. This could mean guiding a younger woman at work, giving tips on how to manage a schedule, or just encouraging someone who feels stuck. By sharing our experiences, we can lift others up. If you see someone who has a skill you lack, you can learn from them too. A healthy community of believers helps each other grow.

Learning New Skills

Sometimes, God might lead us to learn new skills so we can be more effective. This could be a computer course, a new language, or even a cooking class if it helps with a job or home tasks. We should not be afraid to try something new. Age or current position does not have to stop us. If we keep a humble and open mind, we can discover fresh ways to serve God and people around us.

Working Together with a Spouse

For married women, work and goals can be shared topics. If both spouses work outside the home, they need to coordinate schedules and household duties. If one stays home, there should still be respect for each other's contributions. Caring for children and the home is not less important than an office job. Good communication can help a couple support one another's goals. They can pray together about decisions, seek to lighten each other's load, and rejoice in each other's achievements without jealousy.

Times of Job Change

There are seasons when a job ends or changes. Maybe you are forced to quit, or you sense God leading you to start a new business or shift to part-time work. Job changes can be scary, but they can also open new doors. In such times, focus on God's promises. He can provide in unexpected ways. Seek counsel from trusted people, update your skills, and look for opportunities that allow you to stay true to your faith. A change might also be a time to reevaluate your goals and passions.

Finding Contentment

Not everyone will be in a job that matches their dream. Some might long for something different but cannot move yet because of financial or family reasons. Contentment does not mean giving up on growth. It means learning to value the present moment while still looking ahead wisely. Paul, an apostle in the New Testament, said he learned how to be content with a lot or with a little. This attitude can help us see blessings around us each day. It also frees us from envy if we see someone with a better-paying job or a flashier lifestyle.

Serving God Full-Time

Some women might feel led to serve God in a full-time ministry, such as missions, church work, or charitable projects. This is a special calling and can be rewarding. But remember, all work done for God's glory is ministry. A teacher in a public school can be just as much a servant of God as a missionary overseas, if she does her job with love and integrity. The key is to remain faithful and use our gifts to point to God's goodness.

Summary of Practical Steps

1. **Pray Over Your Work**: Invite God into your job or daily tasks. Ask for wisdom and a right attitude.
2. **Plan Goals Wisely**: Make sure your goals honor God, help others, and fit your gifts and limits.
3. **Guard Your Time**: Balance work with rest, family, and personal growth. Set boundaries to prevent burnout.

4. **Honor God in Your Conduct**: Show honesty, kindness, and quality in your work. Avoid unethical actions.
5. **Remember Eternal Values**: Our work is important, but it is not the final measure of our life. We live for a higher purpose.

Conclusion of Chapter 5

Work is part of God's plan for us, whether it is in a high-rise office, a cozy home, or a local community center. It can be a place of growth, service, and joy if we keep our eyes on the Lord. By setting wise goals and doing our tasks with integrity, we can show that our faith is real. We do not rely on job titles or achievements for our identity. We rely on God, who gives us value. At the same time, we aim to do our best, help others, and manage our money and resources responsibly.

When work becomes stressful or dull, we can return to the basics: pray, prioritize, and trust. We can also learn from the examples of women in the Bible who worked diligently and honored God in various roles. There is dignity in every kind of honest work. If we see our labor as a form of service, we can find deeper meaning even in the smallest tasks.

Our goals, too, should be guided by prayer and shaped by godly principles. The path is not always smooth, but God is faithful. He can use our efforts to bless others, care for our families, and shape us to be more like Christ. As we move on to the next chapter, keep in mind that work and friendships often overlap. Our co-workers, neighbors, and friends can all be part of a support system that helps us stay true to God's calling.

CHAPTER 6: FRIENDSHIPS AND SUPPORT

Relationships are a big part of life, and friendships hold a special place. Good friends can lift us when we feel down, laugh with us in happy times, and guide us when we face confusion. The Bible often talks about how important friends can be. In this chapter, we will look at how to build friendships that reflect Christian values, how to be a reliable friend to others, and how to handle problems that sometimes pop up between friends. We will also consider how to form supportive networks in our church and community.

Why Friendships Are Important

1. **Emotional Support**: Friends can share our burdens. They can listen when we have had a rough day or cheer us on when we step into something new. Even a few kind words from a friend can boost our spirits.
2. **Spiritual Growth**: God often uses friends to strengthen our faith. A friend who prays with us or reminds us of Bible truths can help us stay on track. We can learn from each other's insights and experiences.
3. **Practical Help**: Friends can offer real help in daily life. They may bring a meal when we are sick, watch our children in an emergency, or lend a tool when ours breaks. This practical care can build strong bonds.
4. **Shared Joy**: Life has joys that are better when shared. Having a friend to celebrate milestones, birthdays, or small victories can bring an added layer of happiness.

Building Friendships with Intention

Good friendships do not always happen by accident. Sometimes, we must take steps to form them:

1. **Be Friendly**: If we wait for others to come to us, we might wait a long time. A simple smile, greeting, or offer of help can start a connection. If you are in a new environment (like a new church or job), keep an open heart. Introduce yourself to people.
2. **Show Genuine Care**: People can sense when someone is faking interest. If we ask, "How are you doing?" we should listen to the answer. If someone mentions they have a problem, we can follow up later to see how they are coping.
3. **Find Common Ground**: Friendships often form around shared interests or experiences. It could be a hobby like baking, a service project at church, or a group for moms in the neighborhood. Joining such activities can introduce us to new people.
4. **Be Patient**: Deep friendships take time. We should not expect instant closeness. As we spend more time talking, working on projects, or praying together, trust grows. We learn each other's strengths and struggles.

Traits of a Loyal Friend

1. **Honesty**: A loyal friend speaks truth with kindness. They do not flatter or hide what needs to be said. At the same time, they speak gently, not harshly.
2. **Confidentiality**: If a friend shares something personal, a loyal friend keeps it private unless it is a harmful situation where help is needed. Trust is built when we know our personal details will not become gossip.
3. **Dependability**: A loyal friend keeps promises. If they say they will show up, they do their best to be there. Life can be busy, but doing what we say we will do shows respect.
4. **Grace**: Friends should extend grace to each other. We all make mistakes or say the wrong thing sometimes. A loyal friend forgives instead of holding a grudge. This does not mean tolerating abuse, but it does mean showing mercy for normal slips.

Finding Christian Friends

Having friends who share your faith can strengthen your walk with God. They can pray with you, read the Bible with you, and offer advice grounded in Scripture. Here are ways to find such friends:

1. **In Church**: Many friendships begin in local churches. You can attend social events, join a small group, or serve in a ministry where you get to know people better.
2. **Bible Studies**: Some churches or Christian organizations hold Bible studies for women. This can be a safe place to discuss spiritual topics and build friendships.
3. **Conferences and Retreats**: Sometimes, women's events offer a chance to meet believers from different areas. Though these friendships might be long-distance, they can still provide valuable support.
4. **Online Groups**: If you are unable to attend a physical group, you might find online Christian communities. While online interaction should be approached with care, it can still offer encouragement and prayer support.

Remember, while Christian friends are wonderful, do not shut out non-Christian friends. We should maintain connections with people who believe differently. That way, we can show them kindness and share our faith if they are open to it.

Being a Supportive Friend

Friendship is not just about what we receive. It is about giving as well.

1. **Listen Well**: This is one of the greatest gifts we can offer. Put away distractions, make eye contact, and really hear what the other person is saying. Listen for emotions, not just words.
2. **Offer Help**: If a friend is sick, you might cook a meal or run an errand. If they are stressed, you can watch their children for an hour while they rest. Small deeds of service can mean a lot.
3. **Pray Together**: Praying out loud with a friend can feel strange at first, but it can bring you closer. You can keep a list of prayer

requests and updates. This practice also reminds you to lean on God, not just on each other.
4. **Encourage Growth**: A good friend helps you grow as a person. If your friend wants to develop a skill or adopt a healthy habit, you can cheer them on or do it together. If they stray into unwise behavior, a supportive friend gently warns them.

Handling Friendship Conflicts

Conflicts happen even among close friends. We might say something hurtful or fail to be there when needed. The Bible says we should do our best to live in peace with others. Here are some steps:

1. **Talk Directly**: If there is a conflict, do not rely on gossip or silent treatment. Set a time to talk face-to-face if possible. Explain what hurt you, and listen to their perspective.
2. **Speak With Kindness**: Try to avoid name-calling or blaming. Focus on the issue, not the person's character. Say how the action made you feel. Use calm words to keep the conversation respectful.
3. **Apologize if Needed**: If you realize you were wrong, say so and ask for forgiveness. Do not make excuses. A sincere apology can heal many wounds.
4. **Forgive**: True forgiveness is not always easy. It might take time to rebuild trust. But holding a grudge poisons our heart. Letting go of anger frees us to move forward, whether the friendship is fully restored or not.
5. **Set Boundaries**: If a friend continues to act in a harmful way, it may be wise to set some limits. This does not mean hating them, but you might need to reduce contact if they are toxic or refuse to change.

Friendship Seasons

Friendships can change over time. Some friends move away, life stages shift, or interests differ. It can be sad when a close friendship changes or fades, but that is part of life. We can still value what we had and keep the door open for future contact.

1. **Accept Changes**: It might be that you no longer see someone daily, but you can keep in touch with phone calls or messages. Accept that it will not be the same as before, yet you can still care for each other.
2. **Make New Connections**: As time goes on, new friends may step into your life. If you move to a new city or join a new church, do not be afraid to reach out to people. Trust that God can bring new friends at the right time.
3. **Honor Past Friendships**: Even if you lose touch, you can pray for old friends or send a kind note on special occasions. This shows you still care about them, even if your paths no longer cross regularly.

The Influence of Friends

Friends can influence us in many ways—good or bad. The Bible warns that spending time with people who continually encourage harmful behavior can pull us into that behavior. On the other hand, positive friends can inspire us to be better. This does not mean we avoid everyone who struggles. Rather, we need wisdom about our closest friends. If you find that someone constantly leads you away from what is right, it may be time to limit that closeness.

For younger women, peer pressure can be strong. They might face temptations around partying, gossip, or cheating in school. Encouraging them to have good friends can help them stand strong. The same goes for older women dealing with gossip in social groups or pressure in certain circles. The company we keep can either strengthen or weaken our walk with God.

Building Support Networks

A support network is a group of people you can rely on. This can include family members, church friends, neighbors, or mentors. Here are ways to build and maintain a strong support network:

1. **Stay Connected**: Send messages or make calls regularly. Even a quick text can let someone know you care. Do not wait until you have a crisis to talk.
2. **Show Appreciation**: If someone helps you, thank them. Recognize their effort. Appreciation fosters warmth and grows trust over time.
3. **Give and Receive**: A healthy network is not one-sided. You help others when they need it, and you accept help when it is offered. Pride might make us want to handle everything alone, but leaning on others now and then is part of real community.
4. **Look for Mentors**: A mentor is someone who is further along in a certain area of life. This could be a person with a stable marriage if you are newly married, or a woman who has walked with God for many years. Mentors can guide and pray for you. You can also be a mentor to someone else in areas where you have experience.

Friendships in Times of Crisis

When a friend goes through a crisis—like loss, illness, or a big life change—our response can make a big impact. We might feel awkward or unsure what to do. But often, the simplest things help most:

1. **Be Present**: Sometimes just being there means more than any words. Sit with them in the hospital waiting room, or quietly keep them company at home. They may not remember every word you say, but they will remember you were there.
2. **Offer Specific Help**: Instead of saying, "Let me know if you need anything," consider offering something concrete. Ask if you can bring groceries or drive them somewhere. Clear actions can help them during a stressful time.
3. **Pray for Them**: Consistent prayer can bring comfort. You might not be able to fix their situation, but you can ask God to guide them and strengthen them. Let them know you are praying, but avoid empty promises.
4. **Check Back Later**: After a crisis passes, friends often return to their normal routines. But the person may still be grieving or adjusting. A check-in weeks later can show lasting care.

Overcoming Shyness or Past Hurts

Some women hesitate to form new friendships because they are shy or have been hurt in the past. While caution is understandable, staying isolated can lead to loneliness.

1. **Start Small**: Approach one person at a time. A quick chat after church or a brief exchange in a small group can ease you into friendship without overwhelming you.
2. **Set Reasonable Expectations**: Not everyone will become your best friend. Some friendships are casual but still good. Let connections develop naturally.
3. **Seek Healing for Past Hurts**: If old friendships ended in betrayal, you might feel guarded. It can help to talk with a counselor or a wise friend. Healing takes time, but God can restore your ability to trust.
4. **Trust God with Risk**: Making friends always carries some risk of rejection or conflict. Yet, the rewards are worth it. Pray for courage. Trust that God can walk with you, even if some friendships do not work out.

Friendships with People of Different Backgrounds

We live in a diverse world. We might meet people from different cultures, age groups, or social levels. Christians should be open to forming friendships across these lines. We can learn much from people who do not look or speak like us. Also, the Bible says we are all made in God's image. This truth breaks barriers of race, class, or background.

If language is a challenge, we can still share smiles, simple words, or common interests. If we face cultural differences, we can ask polite questions to learn about each other. This openness can lead to rich friendships that show God's love in a divided world.

Technology and Friendships

Online tools can help us keep in touch with friends far away. We can send messages, video chat, or share updates. However, technology should not replace real contact when possible. Also, be cautious about what you share online. Not everyone needs to see every detail of your life. Balance your online interactions with face-to-face time whenever you can. If you use social media, avoid comparing your life to others. Often, people post only their best moments, which can make us feel inferior. Remember that true friendships go deeper than "likes" or filtered pictures.

Friendship and Boundaries

While friendships are good, it is also important to maintain proper boundaries. This can apply to emotional boundaries, time boundaries, and moral boundaries. For example:

- If a friend calls at all hours of the night for non-emergencies, it might be okay to let them know you need rest and will talk at a better time.
- If a friend tries to push you into activities you know are wrong, you must stand firm in your values.
- If you have a friend of the opposite gender and you are married, keep clear lines to protect your marriage. Avoid secret meetings or sharing deep emotional intimacy that belongs to your spouse.

Boundaries do not mean being cold or rude. They mean protecting what is important to keep relationships healthy.

Making Friends in New Seasons of Life

As we go through different stages, our friendship needs may change.

- **New Mothers** might look for other moms to share advice and support.

- **Empty-Nesters** might seek friends who understand the change of having grown children.
- **Retirees** might look for friends who can join them in volunteer or social activities.

In each season, we can ask God to bring people who can walk with us. Sometimes, old friends move into new seasons with us. Other times, we find new friends who relate better to our present stage. Both can be blessings.

Conclusion of Chapter 6

Friendships can bring light into our lives. They help us grow, carry us through hard times, and multiply our joys. As we build friendships, we aim to show honesty, kindness, and faithfulness. We learn to forgive and to ask forgiveness. We also remember that true friendship points us to God, who is our greatest friend of all.

Forming supportive networks is part of healthy Christian living. Whether in a church group, a neighborhood, or an online community, we thrive when we share each other's burdens and joys. It is wise to choose our closest friends carefully, seeking those who encourage us toward good things rather than harmful paths. At the same time, we remain open to connecting with a variety of people from different backgrounds.

If you have felt lonely or disappointed in friendships, know that God cares about your needs. You can ask Him for guidance in finding new friends or reconciling with old ones. Keep in mind that building strong bonds takes time, effort, and sometimes courage. Be patient with yourself and with others. As you move on in your faith, let your friendships be a place where God's love is seen clearly. Support each other, pray for each other, and grow together in wisdom and kindness.

In the next chapters, we will consider more aspects of living with purpose in Christ. We will see how to build inner strength and good habits, and we will also discuss relationships in a deeper way. Keep the truths from this chapter in mind: friendships help shape who we are, so seek God's guidance in choosing and nurturing them. By showing loyalty, honesty, and care, we can form bonds that stand the test of time and challenges.

CHAPTER 7: INNER STRENGTH AND GOOD HABITS

A life built on faith benefits from habits that develop a strong inner character. Women often face duties that demand both emotional and physical strength. Whether it is managing a household, dealing with challenging social settings, or handling personal stress, a steady core can make a big difference. Inner strength allows you to deal with challenges calmly and keep a positive outlook. In this chapter, we will look at ways to form good habits, keep a stable mindset, and rely on God for the power to stand firm. We will also see how small choices each day can lead to big growth over time.

Why Inner Strength Matters

Inner strength involves qualities like courage, patience, resilience, and a sense of peace. It does not mean never feeling weak or never having doubts. Instead, it is about learning to respond wisely when hardships appear. When we have strong roots in our faith, we are less likely to feel crushed by disappointment. Life can be unpredictable, but inner strength helps us keep going without giving up. It also shapes our words and actions, which can bring calm rather than chaos into a home or workplace.

Biblical teaching points out that true strength starts with trusting God. The Bible says that God's power is often displayed when we feel weak. This means we do not have to pretend we have it all together. Instead, we admit our need for God. Then, by building godly habits, we train ourselves to respond in ways that are honorable. The steady framework of daily routines rooted in truth can lead to a calm and thoughtful attitude.

Building Helpful Daily Routines

A routine can help keep life in order and reduce stress. This does not have to be rigid, but having a plan for each day can set the stage for healthy living. Here are some routine ideas:

1. **Morning Quiet Time**: Rising a bit earlier than the rest of the household to read the Bible or pray can center your mind. It sets a peaceful tone before the day's chaos begins.
2. **Scheduled Breaks**: Even if you have a busy job or care for children all day, short pauses can recharge you. A five-minute stretch, a quick step outside, or a brief moment of silence can calm your mind.
3. **Regular Bedtime**: Late nights often lead to tired mornings. Though this might seem small, proper rest makes a big difference in mood and physical energy. Try to keep a consistent bedtime and wake-up schedule if possible.
4. **Task Lists**: Many women juggle responsibilities at home, work, or church. A simple to-do list can help you stay on track. Place the most urgent tasks at the top so you handle them first.
5. **Flexible Family Routines**: If you have children, consider having regular mealtimes or set days for laundry, shopping, or fun activities. Predictable routines can help children feel safe, and they also reduce last-minute rushing.

By forming routines, you create a framework that can handle life's surprises better. When your basic tasks are organized, you can approach challenges with a calmer mind.

Healthy Thoughts and Mindsets

Our inner strength depends a lot on our thought life. Negative self-talk or constant worry can drain our energy. Instead, the Bible teaches us to fix our minds on what is good and true. This involves being aware of our thoughts and choosing to replace harmful thinking with healthy thinking. Here are some tips:

1. **Recognize Harmful Thoughts**: Pay attention to what you say to yourself. Thoughts like "I'm a failure," "I'll never get it right," or "No one cares" can lead to discouragement. The first step is noticing these unhelpful thoughts.
2. **Counter with Truth**: Once you recognize a harmful thought, replace it with a truthful statement. For example, "I can't do

anything right" can be replaced with "I'm learning, and God can guide me." It might feel strange at first, but over time, it can shift your mindset.
3. **Use Scripture Verses**: The Bible is full of verses that remind us of God's presence, our worth in His eyes, and His ability to help us. Memorizing a few verses can arm you with instant truth to combat negative thinking. For instance, Philippians 4:13 says we can do all things through God who gives us strength.
4. **Surround Yourself with Positive Influences**: Spend time with friends who build you up rather than tear you down. Read uplifting books or listen to music that points you to hope rather than despair. This can feed a brighter mindset.

Developing a healthy thought life will not happen overnight. It takes consistent effort and a willingness to rely on God's power. Yet, each small step forward moves you closer to a stable, hopeful outlook.

Physical Health and Its Impact on Inner Strength

Our bodies and minds are linked. Caring for our physical health can boost our mental and emotional resilience. This is not about striving for perfection in appearance. Instead, it is about simple steps that help our bodies feel better, which in turn affects our mood and thinking.

1. **Balanced Eating**: A diet rich in vegetables, fruits, proteins, and whole grains can steady our energy levels. Extreme diets are often not sustainable, but moderate, balanced eating can keep us stronger.
2. **Regular Activity**: Moving your body can reduce stress and improve mood. This might be a brisk walk, a short online exercise class, or gentle stretches. Finding a form of activity you enjoy makes it easier to stay consistent.
3. **Hydration and Rest**: Drinking enough water and getting proper sleep support both body and mind. When we neglect these, we may feel irritable, dizzy, or too tired to handle tasks.
4. **Seek Medical Care if Needed**: Chronic pain or fatigue can lower morale. If you suspect a medical issue, do not hesitate to see a

doctor. Sometimes physical problems can affect our ability to focus on spiritual or emotional matters.

When our bodies feel nurtured, we are more prepared to tackle difficulties. This does not mean we will always be free from health problems, but caring for ourselves can lessen avoidable stress. It also honors God by respecting the body He gave us.

Overcoming Worry and Anxiety

Worry is common among women who manage many things. Anxiety can come from money problems, children's safety, or uncertainty about the future. While some worry is natural, too much can rob us of peace. Inner strength grows when we learn to address anxious thoughts in a constructive way.

1. **Identify the Source**: Write down what is causing fear. Is it a big event? A relationship problem? Noticing the core issue can help you see patterns or triggers.
2. **Pray Specifically**: Instead of letting worries swirl, take them to God. Ask for a solution or for the ability to trust Him if the solution is not clear. Then, thank God for hearing you. This act of trust can bring calm even before the situation changes.
3. **Speak to a Supportive Friend**: Sometimes sharing a worry with a caring person can bring relief. They might offer a fresh viewpoint or just listen. Talking about anxiety can lessen its grip on you.
4. **Practice Relaxation**: Simple methods like slow, deep breathing or quiet reflection can calm racing thoughts. Some people find peace by listening to nature sounds or gentle music while praying.
5. **Limit Media Overload**: Constant exposure to negative news or social media drama can feed anxiety. Setting boundaries on how much you watch or read can help you keep a balanced perspective.

Freedom from worry does not mean ignoring problems, but it does mean trusting God's care while we do our part. Each time we hand our fears over to God, we strengthen our trust muscle, learning that He can hold our concerns.

Self-Discipline and Good Habits

Inner strength often grows through self-discipline. This is not about being strict in a harsh way, but about learning to manage impulses and stay consistent with our commitments. Here are key habits that can build discipline:

1. **Time Management**: Set realistic deadlines for tasks. Use a calendar or an app to track appointments. This can keep you from feeling overwhelmed or forgetting important obligations.
2. **Daily Devotions**: Spending a set time in the Word and prayer each day helps you center your thoughts on God. This can become a habit that shapes your entire attitude. Even a few minutes can make a difference if done consistently.
3. **Avoiding Temptations**: If you are tempted to waste time on certain apps, consider placing a limit on them. If you struggle with unhealthy spending, leave credit cards at home when not needed. Practical steps can help you keep discipline without constant inner battles.
4. **Accountability**: If you have a close friend or family member you trust, share your goals. Knowing someone might ask, "How is that habit going?" can spur you to keep going. This friend can also pray for your self-control.

Self-discipline is a powerful ally for building inner strength. The effort might be challenging at first, but with God's help, the benefits will become clear as you see greater stability and peace in your day-to-day life.

Letting Go of Perfectionism

Some women believe they must be flawless: the perfect mother, the perfect worker, the perfect volunteer. This craving for perfection can actually damage inner strength because it sets an impossible standard. The Bible never commands us to be flawless in daily tasks. Rather, we are called to be faithful and to rely on God's grace.

Perfectionism can lead to burnout, stress, and even strained relationships if we hold others to the same impossible bar. Instead, we can aim for excellence by doing our best while knowing we are finite. We can learn from errors and keep growing. A healthy attitude accepts that we will sometimes fail but can rely on God to guide us and forgive us.

Building Spiritual Muscles

Growing inner strength is similar to exercising a muscle. We do not become spiritually strong by doing nothing. Instead, we strengthen ourselves through practices rooted in God's Word:

1. **Memorizing Scripture**: Learning verses by heart gives you quick access to truth during tough moments. Repetition can help cement these words in your mind. This is helpful when you cannot open a Bible right away.
2. **Fasting with Wisdom**: Some Christians set aside periods of time to fast from certain foods or activities for spiritual focus. This is not a way to impress God, but a method to train ourselves in self-control and to devote more time to prayer.
3. **Serving Others**: Helping people in need can build compassion and humility. It also trains us to look beyond ourselves, which contributes to stronger character.
4. **Regular Worship**: Attending church consistently or worshiping at home with family can ground us in God's truth. Singing praises and hearing the Word preached shapes our perspective and helps us stand firm.

As we do these things, we become more steady. It is like slowly lifting heavier weights each time. We might not notice the change day by day, but over weeks and months, our spiritual core grows.

Developing Patience

Patience is a big part of inner strength. When we lack patience, we become irritated quickly. We might lash out in anger or rush into poor decisions.

Patience means waiting without getting bitter. It also means giving people space to grow rather than demanding instant change.

1. **Pause Before Reacting**: If someone says or does something that upsets you, pause. Take a breath. Pray a quick prayer for calm. That short moment can keep you from saying something you will regret.
2. **Remember God's Patience with Us**: The Bible shows us that God is slow to anger, giving people many chances to repent. When we remember how patient God is with us, it becomes easier to be patient with others.
3. **Plan for Delays**: If you know traffic will be heavy, leave earlier. If you know your child takes time to get ready, build that into your schedule. Reducing the chance for rushed pressure can protect your peace.
4. **Look for Teachable Moments**: If you lead a team or care for children, patience can be a tool to help them learn. Instead of jumping in to fix every mistake, guide them so they can figure things out. This fosters growth in them and in you.

Patience is not weakness. It is the ability to remain calm and gracious under stress. Over time, this fosters stronger bonds and a more peaceful environment.

Standing Firm in Values

Inner strength also shows when you stand by your principles, even if others disagree. Peer pressure can be a real challenge, whether at work, among social circles, or even at family gatherings. Standing firm requires a mix of courage and wisdom.

1. **Know Your Convictions**: Take time to figure out which beliefs are non-negotiable for you. This should be rooted in biblical teaching. When you are clear on your convictions, it is easier to stay steady under pressure.
2. **Communicate Calmly**: If someone challenges your stance, respond politely. Yelling or insulting does not help. A firm but gentle explanation can show that you respect the person yet will not compromise your beliefs.

3. **Accept Consequences**: Sometimes standing firm has a price. You might lose a friendship or face disapproval. In those moments, recall that pleasing God is more important than pleasing people. God sees and cares when we choose what is right over what is popular.
4. **Find Allies**: Look for people who share your values. They can encourage you when you feel alone. You can also encourage them, creating a support system of shared convictions.

Standing for truth in a loving way is part of what inner strength looks like. It does not mean forcing your beliefs on others. It means not bending who you are to fit in.

Overcoming Past Hurts

Past hurts or failures can weaken our sense of self. We might feel stuck or unworthy because of what happened long ago. Inner strength requires addressing these wounds rather than ignoring them.

1. **Admit the Pain**: Denying past hurts will not make them go away. Being honest with yourself and with God is a first step toward healing. If needed, speak with a counselor or a trusted friend.
2. **Forgive and Release**: This can be challenging. Forgiveness does not mean saying the hurt was okay; it means letting go of anger and leaving judgment to God. Holding onto resentment drains emotional energy and keeps us bound.
3. **Learn from Mistakes**: If the hurt involves a mistake you made, acknowledge it and seek God's forgiveness. Then learn what you can from it. Mistakes can become stepping stones for growth if we handle them in a healthy way.
4. **Stay Hopeful**: Past pain does not define your future. The Bible says God can bring good from what was meant for harm. While you cannot change the past, you can move forward with renewed hope, trusting God's plan.

Working through past hurts might take time, and it may involve setbacks. Yet, with God's grace and a steady willingness to heal, you can gain a deeper strength that grows out of the lessons learned.

Learning to Rest

In a world that values constant activity, many women feel guilty if they take time to rest. However, true rest is not laziness. It is necessary for maintaining strength in mind and body.

1. **Sabbath Principle**: The idea of resting one day out of seven is based on God's pattern in creation. Though modern life might not allow a full day off each week, the principle is still relevant. Try to set aside regular periods of downtime.
2. **Disconnect from Devices**: Constant phone alerts and social media updates can keep your brain on high alert. Turning off notifications for a while can give your mind space to breathe.
3. **Do Something Peaceful**: Rest can be as simple as taking a slow walk, reading a comforting book, or sitting quietly in the yard. Choose a calm activity that helps you detach from stress.
4. **Pray for Peace**: Invite God into your rest. Thank Him for the good things in your life and ask Him to renew your energy. This can keep rest from turning into mere idleness.

Regular rest restores our mental and physical reserves. It also shows our trust in God's provision. We do not have to handle everything nonstop. Stepping back refreshes us for the tasks ahead.

The Power of Gratitude

Another key part of inner strength is gratitude. A thankful heart notices blessings, even in tough times. This does not mean ignoring real problems. Rather, it means choosing to focus on the good gifts present in each day.

1. **Keep a Thankfulness Journal**: Write down a few things you are thankful for daily. This habit can train your mind to spot blessings rather than dwell on irritations.
2. **Thank Others**: People in your life might be doing small acts of kindness every day. Saying thanks to them builds a habit of appreciation. It also lifts their spirits.
3. **Reflect on God's Goodness**: Before sleep, recall moments of grace in your day. It could be a safe drive, a warm meal, or a kind word

from a friend. Acknowledging these moments helps you go to bed with a sense of peace.
4. **Speak Grateful Words**: Let your speech reflect a grateful heart. This might include sharing testimonies of how God has helped you. When you speak about good things, it can encourage those around you.

Gratitude has a way of lightening burdens. While life is not perfect, noticing God's mercies helps us keep a balanced perspective. This perspective fuels resilience.

Keeping a Bigger Perspective

Focusing on our daily tasks or personal struggles can sometimes narrow our view. We might forget the bigger story God is writing. Remembering that God has a grand plan can boost our inner strength. Our small actions and faithfulness fit into His design.

1. **Reflect on God's Promises**: The Bible contains promises about God's support, final justice, and eternal life. Keeping these in mind reminds us that current troubles are not the full picture.
2. **Serve Beyond Yourself**: Engaging in acts of service for others can pull us out of self-focus. It reminds us that the world is bigger than our personal concerns. This can strengthen our character by letting us see the impact of kindness.
3. **Pray About Global Issues**: While we cannot fix everything, praying for people in other places widens our heart. We realize God is working all around the world, and we are part of a global family of believers.
4. **Trust in Eternal Hope**: Even if certain problems never resolve in this life, Christians believe in an eternal future with God. This hope can steady us when events seem unfair or painful.

Keeping this broader outlook reduces panic about daily troubles. We see that our challenges fit into a greater context where God's purpose prevails. That awareness helps us stand firm.

Conclusion of Chapter 7

Developing inner strength and good habits is a process that unfolds over time. Each small decision—a few minutes of prayer, a kind response instead of an angry one, a healthy meal choice, or a short break from work—can build a foundation of resilience. Rather than chasing some form of external perfection, we rely on God's guidance to shape us from the inside. Our thoughts, routines, and attitudes all work together to create a stable sense of well-being that honors Him.

This chapter covered key steps such as forming routines, watching our thoughts, taking care of our bodies, practicing patience, and standing firm in values. We also looked at the importance of rest, gratitude, and a bigger perspective. Though life can be unpredictable, these practices anchor us in truth and help us handle ups and downs more calmly.

As we move forward in this book, we will see how our inner strength and habits connect to how we relate to others and how we honor God in daily living. A firm interior life makes it easier to navigate relationships and keep a clean conscience. By continuing to apply what we have discussed here, you will be better prepared for the next areas of growth that lie ahead.

CHAPTER 8: RELATIONSHIPS AND HOLY LIVING

Relationships form a big part of our lives, whether they are with family, friends, coworkers, or neighbors. We also have a relationship with ourselves, based on how we view our worth and conduct. As Christian women, we want our relationships to reflect God's character. This does not mean we will never have conflicts or struggles, but we aim to treat others with kindness and honor God's standards in our conduct. In this chapter, we will look at principles for holy living in the context of different relationships, including marriage and single life. We will also explore how to maintain moral boundaries and extend love in a truthful way.

Understanding Holy Living

Holy living means living in a way that is set apart for God's purposes. It is a lifestyle that strives to meet God's moral standards, guided by the Bible. This does not make us superior to others. Rather, it involves humility and obedience. At its core, holy living invites us to respect God, respect ourselves, and respect other people. When our relationships rest on these principles, we build an atmosphere of trust and genuine care.

In practical terms, holy living affects how we handle feelings such as anger, how we speak to others, how we manage our desires, and how we use our free time. It also shapes our sense of right and wrong. If we are married, it influences how we honor our spouse. If we are single, it influences how we use our time and maintain moral boundaries. In every case, it points us to a path of sincerity rather than selfish gain.

Love and Truth in Relationships

The Bible teaches us to love others, but love does not mean approving everything they do. Real love often includes honesty and clear boundaries.

For example, you can love a friend who makes poor choices without praising those choices. You can still show kindness while gently warning them about harmful outcomes. Similarly, if a person is disrespectful to you, you can remain respectful yourself, but you do not need to pretend their actions are correct.

Loving in truth also means we do not manipulate or deceive. We strive to be trustworthy. This can be tested in stressful moments, but maintaining honesty builds a secure bond with others. Whether in marriage, friendships, or with neighbors, truth and love together create a balanced connection.

Marriage and Commitment

For women who are married, the Bible portrays marriage as a sacred bond. The aim is a loving partnership where both spouses help each other grow closer to God. A few key principles can guide married life:

1. **Respect and Support**: Each spouse should treat the other with honor. This includes listening before speaking, supporting each other's goals, and speaking positively rather than tearing one another down.
2. **Faithfulness**: Staying true to one's spouse physically and emotionally is important. This includes being mindful of how we spend time alone with people of the opposite sex and keeping healthy boundaries to avoid temptations.
3. **Selflessness**: Marriage can become strained if one spouse always demands their way. Learning to serve each other's needs can build a deeper bond. This does not mean losing your voice or desires. Instead, it means finding healthy compromise and giving space for both partners to grow.
4. **Shared Values**: If both partners share a love for God's Word, they can pray together, make decisions based on the Bible, and handle stress with a sense of unity. If a husband or wife is not a believer, the believing spouse can still be a light through consistent kindness and patience.

5. **Handling Conflict**: Disagreements happen. The goal is to face them constructively—listening, apologizing if needed, and seeking solutions that consider both views. Dragging in old grievances or using harsh language can damage trust over time.

While no marriage is perfect, couples who practice these principles often find greater harmony. They also model to others what a loving, God-centered union looks like. If troubles arise, wise counsel from a pastor or a trusted counselor can help bring healing.

Single Life and Service

For women who are not married, holy living has its own form. Singleness can be a chance to serve in unique ways. Without the responsibilities of a spouse or children, single women might have more time to volunteer, focus on community projects, or mentor younger people. The Bible gives examples of single individuals who did significant work for God. This reminds us that marriage is not required to live a meaningful or holy life.

At the same time, single women might face pressures or loneliness. They might worry about the future. Maintaining moral boundaries in dating relationships can also be a test. Here are some points to consider:

1. **Find Purpose**: A single woman can still have a strong purpose, whether in ministry, career, or community service. Focus on the opportunities God has given you right now.
2. **Stay Connected**: Avoid isolation. Building healthy friendships and joining church activities can prevent loneliness. A supportive circle can also help you maintain wise choices in relationships.
3. **Dating with Standards**: If you choose to date, be clear about boundaries. Aim to honor God in physical and emotional closeness. If a person pressures you to act against your values, they may not be the right match for you.
4. **Seek God for Fulfillment**: While marriage can be wonderful, it is not the sole source of joy. A single season (or life) can still be full of blessings, friendships, and ways to bless others. Drawing near to God can fill emotional gaps that no human can meet.

Holy living for singles involves trusting God's plan, staying pure in conduct, and using the season of singleness for good works. Whether you remain single or later marry, honoring God in each stage brings peace.

Boundaries in Close Relationships

Boundaries help keep relationships healthy. Sometimes people mix up love with the idea of allowing anything. In truth, boundaries can protect both parties. If someone is consistently overstepping your limits—verbally or physically—you can calmly but firmly say that you do not accept that behavior. This is not unloving; it is wise and can prompt healthier patterns or reveal if the person is unwilling to change.

Examples of boundaries include:

- **Time Boundaries**: Deciding how much time you can give to a person who might rely heavily on you.
- **Emotional Boundaries**: Not taking responsibility for another adult's emotions. You can care without letting them control your feelings or manipulate you.
- **Physical Boundaries**: Protecting your personal space or body from unwanted contact.
- **Moral Boundaries**: Sticking to your convictions about right and wrong, even if someone urges you to cross them.

Setting boundaries can feel awkward, but it prevents more serious problems later. It also helps maintain respect in the relationship.

Handling Toxic or Abusive Situations

Holy living does not mean staying silent if you are in harm's way. If someone is abusive—physically or emotionally—you have the right to seek safety. This might mean leaving the environment or involving trusted authorities. Churches should never teach that a woman must endure violence to keep up an image of being "holy." True holiness values life and well-being, and it recognizes that abuse destroys the bond of trust in a relationship. If this situation applies to you or someone you know, look for help from counselors, support lines, or church leaders who understand the seriousness of abuse.

Friendships and Holy Living

While friendships may not have the same commitment level as marriage or dating, holy living still applies. This means speaking truthfully, not joining in gossip or backbiting, and being considerate of each other's boundaries. If a friend pressures you to adopt habits that go against your convictions, you can speak honestly. If the pressure continues, you might have to limit that friendship or end it. True friends will respect your standards, even if they do not share them.

Also, you can be a positive influence on friends who are seeking truth. By living in line with your beliefs—treating others well, managing anger responsibly, showing kindness—you reflect God's character. You can also invite friends to church activities or share your faith gently when they are open to it. Holy living should not make us distant or judgmental; it should help us become a steady source of warmth and honesty.

Speech and Communication

Our words reveal what is in our hearts. Speaking in a way that honors God involves honesty, respect, and a refusal to tear people down. This can be a big challenge when emotions run high. A few guidelines can help:

1. **Avoid Harsh Criticism**: If you have a concern, phrase it in a calm way. Insults or name-calling do not solve problems. They only stir up anger.
2. **Speak With Respect**: Even in disagreement, treat the other person with dignity. This does not mean surrendering your viewpoint, but it does mean addressing them politely.

3. **Skip Gossip**: Talking behind someone's back can destroy trust and damage reputations. If you have an issue, address it directly or let it go. Gossip rarely solves anything.
4. **Encourage**: Look for ways to build others up. A kind word can spark hope. If a friend or family member does something praiseworthy, mention it. Encouragement can brighten their day and strengthen your relationship.
5. **Listen More**: Good communication is not just about talking. Listening to understand rather than just waiting to speak can prevent misunderstandings. It also shows respect for the person you are with.

Developing thoughtful speech requires practice. We might catch ourselves speaking hastily or making critical remarks. By noticing and correcting these habits, we can grow in maturity and respect.

Honoring God in Work Relationships

Holy living is not limited to family and close friends. It extends to the workplace and community. We reflect God's standard by being honest, working diligently, and refraining from badmouthing colleagues. If a conflict arises with a boss or coworker, we can try to resolve it calmly or seek proper channels if it cannot be fixed through a simple chat.

If you face unethical practices at work, you might need to refuse to participate or even change jobs. That can be a tough decision, but sticking to godly values matters more than keeping a position through dishonesty. Over time, people may recognize you as someone who can be trusted. This can open doors for you to share your faith or be a positive leader.

Modesty and Presentation

Holy living also touches on how we present ourselves, including clothing and appearance. Modesty does not mean dressing in a drab way. It means dressing in a way that respects yourself and others. The goal is not to draw inappropriate attention or cause temptation. There is room for individual preference, but the key question is: "Does my clothing show self-respect and consideration for those around me?" This approach is not about policing women's fashion choices in a harsh manner. It is about a thoughtful, self-respecting attitude that aims to reflect dignity.

Sexual Purity

In a culture that often pushes casual intimacy, the Bible's teaching on sexual purity can feel countercultural. However, Christians believe that sexual activity is designed for the bond of marriage. Outside of that bond, it can create emotional damage, guilt, or heartbreak. Maintaining purity involves practical decisions:

1. **Accountability**: If you are dating, consider group settings or having a friend you can check in with about temptations.
2. **Avoid Risky Situations**: Do not place yourself in settings that make it easy to cross moral lines. Be wise about late nights alone or substance use that lowers self-control.
3. **Engage Your Mind**: Purity is not just physical; it is also in our thoughts. Being cautious about the media we consume and how we fantasize can protect our inner life.
4. **Seek Forgiveness if Needed**: If you have failed in this area, remember that God is full of mercy. Confess sincerely, turn from the behavior, and accept the healing He offers. The Bible shows many cases of individuals who found forgiveness and new paths after wrongdoing.

Sexual purity is not about shaming people. It is about respecting yourself, your future (or present) spouse, and God's plan. If we stumble, God's grace is available, and we can choose to live differently going forward.

Forgiveness in Relationships

Holy living cannot happen without forgiveness. In any relationship, conflicts and hurts are bound to occur. Forgiving does not mean condoning harmful actions, but it does mean releasing the grudge and letting God handle the final judgment. Holding onto bitterness poisons our own hearts. When we choose to let go, we free ourselves to move forward.

1. **Acknowledge the Offense**: Pretending it did not happen only leads to hidden anger. Recognize the hurt, then decide to forgive.
2. **Pray for the Person**: This might be tough, but praying for the one who wronged you can soften your heart. It also reminds you that they are human and in need of God's help, just as we all are.
3. **Set Boundaries if Needed**: Forgiveness does not always mean staying close to someone who is toxic. In some cases, you can forgive but still keep healthy distance.
4. **Forgive Yourself Too**: Sometimes the hardest person to forgive is ourselves. If you have done something you regret, bring it to God. Accept His pardon. Holding onto self-directed anger can keep you stuck.

Practicing forgiveness helps maintain a pure heart. It opens the way for healing in relationships and can lead to reconciliation if the other person also chooses to change.

Serving Others with Integrity

Holy living in relationships also calls us to serve others with genuine intent. Whether it is helping a neighbor, volunteering at church, or supporting a family member, our hearts should be focused on caring, not on seeking praise. This is part of the humility that marks a life devoted to God. When we serve quietly and faithfully, God sees our efforts. We can pray for the people we assist, asking God to bless them and to use our small acts of kindness for good.

At times, we may be tempted to show off our service. But the Bible teaches that it is better to serve in a quiet way than to make a big display. If we do our good works only to gain attention, we lose sight of the deeper reason for service—love for God and for His people. Serving with integrity means acting out of compassion, not out of a desire for recognition.

Raising Children in Holy Living

For mothers, an important aspect of holy living is teaching children about God's ways. This starts with setting an example at home. Children watch how parents speak, handle stress, and treat others. Regularly reading the Bible together, praying for needs, and guiding them to do what is right helps create an environment where they learn godly values. Correcting them in love, rather than anger, also models the character of God.

This does not guarantee perfect outcomes, as children have their own choices. Still, showing them consistent grace, teaching them moral standards, and letting them see real faith in action can plant seeds that remain with them for life. Even if they wander, those seeds can draw them back to truth later. Parenting is a major area where relationships and holy living blend in daily practice.

Overcoming Struggles with Envy or Comparison

In relationships, envy can creep in when we see someone else's success or happiness. Comparison can make us feel either prideful (if we think we are better) or inadequate (if we think we are worse). Neither attitude matches holy living. A better approach is to be thankful for our own blessings and to rejoice with those who are blessed. We can learn from others' strengths without resenting them.

If you notice envy stirring in your heart, pray for that person's well-being. Thank God for what He is doing in their life. Then remember ways God has been good to you. This shift in perspective can break envy's hold. Over time, you can develop a mindset that is quick to be glad for others while resting in the path God has given you.

Conclusion of Chapter 8

Holy living is a wide topic that touches every relationship we have—marriage, single life, friendship, work, church, and more. It stems from a heart dedicated to God's standards, which includes love, truth, purity, and forgiveness. Whether you are married or single, you can walk in ways that reflect God's character. Whether you are raising children or focusing on a career, you can maintain moral integrity. Whether you are dealing with easy friendships or navigating toxic situations, you can ask God for wisdom and set wise boundaries.

By practicing these principles, we shine a light in our communities. People may notice our peace, our honesty, and our compassion. They might even ask what motivates us to live differently. That can open doors to share about the hope we have in Jesus. As you move on, keep these points in mind:

- Holy living is about honoring God's standards, not earning His love.
- Relationships thrive on truth, respect, and sincere care.
- Boundaries protect the well-being of everyone involved.
- Forgiveness is central to avoiding resentment and living with a clean heart.
- Each stage of life—married or single—offers a way to serve God and others.

In the next chapters, we will keep building on this foundation. We have explored how to develop inner strength, good habits, and moral living in our relationships. As we continue, we will look at other topics that help women find a stable sense of joy and purpose in Christ. Stay encouraged and remember that God is your guide. If you have felt convicted or challenged, that can be a sign of growth. Keep relying on God's Word and the support of fellow believers as you move forward in faith.

CHAPTER 9: OVERCOMING WORRY AND FEAR

Worry and fear can take hold of our minds in many ways. A woman might worry about her family, her health, her finances, or events in the world. Fear can rob us of sleep, peace, and even the desire to move forward. Yet, the Bible tells us again and again not to be afraid. In this chapter, we will look at what causes worry and fear, how these feelings can affect our lives, and how to handle them in a practical, godly way. We will also look at examples from the Bible and real life, showing how trust in God can calm the heart.

---

1. Why Worry and Fear Appear

1.1 Uncertainty About the Future
One main cause of worry is not knowing what lies ahead. Will we have enough money? Will our children make wise decisions? Will our health hold up as we get older? These questions can circle in our thoughts day and night. While planning and thinking ahead are wise, if we focus too much on the unknown, we can fall into anxiety.

1.2 Past Traumas or Bad Experiences
Some people carry fear because of difficult events from the past. A painful event can color how we see the present and future. If someone faced serious hardship or loss, they may be extra cautious, fearing that bad events will repeat.

1.3 Heavy Pressures and Expectations
Women often shoulder many responsibilities. They may feel required to take care of children, maintain a home, help extended family, and also succeed at work. The pressure to do it all can lead to fear of failure. Worry creeps in when we think we must meet every demand without error.

1.4 Media Overload
Constantly seeing bad news on television or online can feed worry. We see crime reports, health scares, and global conflicts. While staying informed

can be good, too much negative information can build a spirit of fear if we do not set limits.

---

2. Effects of Worry and Fear

2.1 Strain on the Mind and Body
When we worry, we might feel tense, lose sleep, or have trouble focusing. Long-term anxiety can affect our bodies, leading to headaches, digestive problems, or fatigue. In severe cases, it can bring on panic attacks or chronic stress.

2.2 Damaged Relationships
Worry and fear can push us to act in ways that harm our connections with others. We might become overly controlling, suspicious, or withdrawn. Friends and family may feel shut out or even hurt by our anxious behaviors. Communication can break down when fear drives our words.

2.3 Spiritual Barriers
Constant fear can crowd out trust in God. Instead of turning to Him, we might obsess over possible dangers. This does not mean we lose our faith entirely, but fear can make it harder to sense God's peace. We might skip prayer time or Bible reading because our thoughts are stuck on worst-case scenarios.

2.4 Missed Opportunities
Fear can freeze us in place. We might not try new things or accept responsibilities that God wants us to take on. A woman who is scared of failing might pass up a chance to lead a project, learn a new skill, or share her faith with a neighbor.

---

3. Biblical Insights on Fear

3.1 "Do Not Be Afraid"
Scripture contains many reminders to avoid fear. One often-quoted verse is Isaiah 41:10, which says not to fear because God is with us. This is not a

casual command. It is a reassurance that God is bigger than our problems. When the Bible repeats a command often, it is a sign that we need to pay special attention.

3.2 Stories of People Who Faced Fear

- **Moses**: He was nervous about leading the Israelites out of slavery. He felt unfit to speak to Pharaoh. But God promised to be with him, and Moses learned to trust that promise.
- **Esther**: She feared for her life when she had to speak to the king on behalf of her people. By trusting in God's plan, she gathered her courage and saved many lives.
- **David**: He faced giant threats, literally and spiritually. He wrote songs (Psalms) about his fears and how he trusted in God to rescue him.

These examples show that fear itself is not unusual. What matters is how we respond. Each of these people brought their fears to God, found courage, and moved ahead despite the risks.

3.3 Trust vs. Fear

A key principle in the Bible is that trust in God replaces fear. This does not mean we ignore common sense or deny real dangers. Instead, trust means we see God's power and love as bigger than the problem. Psalm 56:3-4 says that when we are afraid, we can put our trust in God. His character and promises form a firm foundation, even when storms gather.

---

4. Practical Steps to Handle Worry

4.1 Name the Fear

Write down exactly what you fear. Is it a health issue? A job insecurity? An issue with a child? Getting specific helps you see what you are really facing. Sometimes, vague worry is worse than identifying the actual concern.

4.2 Pray with Honesty

Bring that specific fear to God in prayer. Tell Him how you feel. Ask Him for help, wisdom, and peace. Some people find it helpful to pray out loud or to journal their prayers. Honesty removes the mask and allows God to speak to our true concerns.

4.3 Plan Wisely
If your fear is related to a practical area—like finances—make a plan. Look at your budget, see where expenses can be reduced, or consider new job options. If you fear an upcoming medical test, get the information you need and ask the doctor questions. Doing something constructive can lower anxiety because you feel less helpless.

4.4 Seek Wise Counsel
Sometimes we need an outside perspective. Talk to a friend, pastor, or mentor. They might see an angle you missed or have gone through a similar struggle. Hearing someone else's view can lessen your sense of isolation.

4.5 Replace Negative Thoughts
Catch yourself when negative "what if" thoughts arise. Counter them with words like, "Even if this problem is real, I can trust God to give me strength," or "God has helped me before, and He can help me again." This mental shift does not solve everything instantly, but it trains your mind to break free from the cycle of worry.

---

5. Spiritual Habits to Fight Fear

5.1 Consistent Bible Reading
When we fill our minds with Scripture, we see how God provided for His people in the past. We learn about His promises and character. Over time, this can reshape how we face our own troubles. Focus on passages that highlight God's care.

5.2 Focused Prayer Times
Rather than letting worries steal your attention all day, plan times to talk with God about your fears. This might be in the morning or before bed. Knowing you have a set time to address these concerns can keep them from dominating every moment.

5.3 Worship and Praise
Singing or listening to worship music can shift your heart from fear to

gratitude. Praise reminds us that God is powerful and worthy of trust. Even if you do not sing publicly, you can hum a hymn while doing tasks or quietly meditate on God's greatness.

5.4 Fellowship with Believers
Spending time with other Christians who have faced fear and found peace in God can lift your spirits. Sharing testimonies of God's help can spark hope. Group prayer, Bible studies, or small gatherings can be places to encourage one another.

---

6. Addressing Common Fears

6.1 Fear of Rejection
Many women worry about what others think. They fear not being accepted by friends, co-workers, or even family. This can push them to avoid new situations or hide their true thoughts.

- **Truth**: Our worth comes from God, not from people's approval. If someone rejects us for living a life of faith or for having certain standards, that is not a measure of our real value.

6.2 Fear of Failure
This can show up in both big goals and small tasks. Fear of failure might stop a woman from starting a new business, teaching a class at church, or going back to school.

- **Truth**: Failure can be a teacher. Even if plans do not go as we hoped, God can use the experience to grow our wisdom. We do our best, but we leave the results to Him.

6.3 Fear of the Unknown
Not knowing how events will turn out can lead to worry. Moving to a new city, changing jobs, or facing an unexpected shift in life can bring anxiety.

- **Truth**: God knows the future and has promised to guide us step by step. He does not show us the entire path at once, but He gives enough light for the next step.

6.4 Fear for Children
Mothers can worry deeply about their kids' health, choices, and future. This can become a constant burden if not balanced with trust.

- **Truth**: While parents should care and guide, the ultimate outcome is in God's hands. Praying for children is powerful. Setting wise rules is good. But children grow and make their own choices. God's reach extends beyond our own abilities.

---

7. Small Daily Changes for Less Worry

7.1 Limit Media Input
As mentioned earlier, too much negative news can fuel worry. Try setting a limit on how many minutes per day you spend reading or watching news. Focus on reliable sources and skip sensational stories that aim to provoke fear.

7.2 Keep a Thankful Record
Some women keep a notebook where they list blessings each day—things that went right, kind words received, or tasks completed successfully. This can remind you of good things happening and reduce worry.

7.3 Simplify Schedules
An overloaded calendar can heighten worry. Look at your commitments. Is there anything you can drop or postpone? Leaving margin in your schedule can make you feel more relaxed. It also gives time to handle unexpected issues without panic.

7.4 Practice Slow Breathing
When panic rises, take a few slow, deep breaths. Inhale for a count of four, hold for a count of four, exhale for a count of four. This can steady your nerves and help you think more clearly.

8. God's Strength in Our Weakness

8.1 Weakness Is Not Shameful
Sometimes women feel they must appear strong, never showing fear. But the Bible says God's power shows up best when we know we are weak. This truth means we do not have to fake confidence. We can admit, "I'm afraid," and ask God to step in. That moment of humility can open the door to real help.

8.2 Leaning on God's Promises
God has promised never to leave us or forsake us. He promises that those who call on His name will find help in times of trouble. These are more than words on a page; they represent the faithful nature of God. When we feel overwhelmed by fear, reminding ourselves of these promises can restore hope.

8.3 Finding Peace in Prayer
Philippians 4:6-7 says that when we bring our requests to God with thanks, His peace will guard our hearts and minds. The word "guard" suggests a protective barrier. Worry might keep trying to push in, but God's peace is like a shield. It does not mean we ignore real problems, but it means we have an inner calm that stands firm against panic.

---

9. Overcoming Specific Scenarios

9.1 Financial Struggles
Financial worries are common. If bills stack up or income is uncertain, fear can grip the heart. Planning a budget, seeking advice from those who manage money well, or even talking to a professional can bring clarity.

- **Spiritual Step**: Ask God for daily bread, as the Lord's Prayer teaches. Trust that He cares about your basic needs.

9.2 Health Concerns
A frightening diagnosis or even the risk of illness can create fear. While seeking doctors, remember that God is still the ultimate healer.

- **Spiritual Step**: Ask others to pray with you. Sometimes just knowing friends and church members are praying can lift the burden of fear.

9.3 Relationship Breakdowns
Fear can arise when a marriage or close friendship is strained. We might worry about being alone or rejected.

- **Spiritual Step**: Focus on communication. Seek counseling if needed. Trust that God can bring healing, but also be willing to forgive or change if that is needed.

10. Trust Grows Through Trials

10.1 Building Inner Faith
Times of worry can actually strengthen faith if we choose to lean on God rather than pull away. It may feel unnatural at first, but each little decision to pray, to hold onto Scripture, or to reach out for help can reinforce a deeper trust.

10.2 Learning from Others' Stories
Hearing testimonies of how others overcame fear can spark your own hope. You can find such accounts in Christian books, at church, or by talking to people in your community. They might share how they faced job loss, illness, or heartbreak, yet found God faithful.

10.3 Celebrating Milestones
(We will avoid using the word you asked us not to.) Instead, we acknowledge small successes. When a period of fear passes and you see how God carried you, take a moment to thank Him. This memory can serve you the next time worry knocks on your door.

11. Continuous Growth in Trust

11.1 Not a One-Time Fix
Overcoming worry is often a process. You might find relief, then face a new

fear weeks or months later. That does not mean you have failed. It means you continue to apply what you have learned, leaning on God again and again.

11.2 Helping Others
When you have learned to manage fear in a certain area, you can support someone else who is going through a similar challenge. Even a listening ear or a simple prayer can give them strength to keep going.

11.3 Staying Humble
Pride can make us think, "I shouldn't be afraid. I should be tougher than this." But humility says, "I am human. I need God." Recognizing this need is the gateway to His help.

---

12. Action Points for a Fear-Less Life

Let us summarize some clear, actionable points to combat worry:

1. **Identify the fear in writing**: This uncovers the real issue.
2. **Pray honestly**: Speak out your fears to God.
3. **Seek solutions**: If there is a practical step you can take, do it.
4. **Limit negativity**: Turn down the volume on news or sources that amplify fear.
5. **Rely on a support network**: Friends, church groups, or mentors can pray and encourage.
6. **Keep your mind filled with God's promises**: Read or memorize Scripture that addresses fear.
7. **Practice gratitude**: List blessings to shift focus away from panic.
8. **Allow for rest**: Adequate sleep and downtime reduce stress.
9. **Celebrate small breakthroughs**: When you sense progress, thank God. (Again, avoiding that certain word by using "acknowledge" or "be thankful for.")

---

13. Conclusion of Chapter 9

Worry and fear are not easy to shake off. They can appear at any moment and might cling to our thoughts. However, God's Word speaks clearly: we do not have to remain trapped by fear. Through prayer, Scripture, wise planning, and supportive friends, we can learn to quiet those anxious voices. Real peace is possible, not because we have no problems, but because we know the One who holds us.

It does not matter if your worry is big or small. God cares. He can replace panic with peace and turn dread into trust. Each time we choose to lean on Him, we take another step toward a life less ruled by fear. Over time, we can see that He is indeed faithful, carrying us through storms and guiding us through uncertainties. This shift in perspective frees us to live in hope rather than in dread.

As you close this chapter, consider any specific areas in your life where fear might be gaining ground. Let God's promises shine into that place. Speak with Him plainly about it. Seek a friend's prayer support if you can. And remember that learning to rest in God's care is a day-by-day process. Little by little, He will show you that He is stronger than any fear you face.

CHAPTER 10: STUDYING SCRIPTURE CAREFULLY

Reading the Bible is a cornerstone of Christian life. It is where we learn about God's ways, His plan for humanity, and His promises. Yet, many women feel unsure about how to study Scripture in a deep way. They might read random verses, not knowing how to apply them. In this chapter, we will explore practical methods for studying the Bible carefully, so we can grow in wisdom and gain confidence in God's truth. We will also talk about common mistakes and how to avoid them, as well as how to fit serious Bible study into a busy schedule.

---

1. Why Careful Study Matters

1.1 Learning God's Character
The Bible is more than a history book. It reveals who God is: His love, His holiness, His patience, and His power. Without careful reading, we might miss these vital parts of His nature. A quick glance might not show how each passage ties into the bigger picture of God's plan.

1.2 Guiding Our Decisions
Scripture offers wisdom for daily life. Topics include money, relationships, work, and personal integrity. A casual, surface-level reading might overlook the depth of guidance available. By digging in with attention, we can uncover truths that shape our actions.

1.3 Preventing Misunderstandings
Taken out of context, a single verse can be misunderstood. This can lead to confusion or even harmful teachings. Proper study techniques help us see the original setting and intent behind each part of the Bible, lowering the risk of errors.

1.4 Feeding Our Faith
Like physical food nourishes the body, the Bible nourishes the soul. Thoughtful study can strengthen our trust in God, giving us a stable

foundation. When troubles arise, the knowledge of Scripture can comfort and direct us.

2. Preparing Our Hearts

2.1 Pray First
Before you open the Bible, pause for a short prayer. Ask God to help you understand and to change you with His truth. This simple habit can shift your mindset from just reading words to seeking a living message from God.

2.2 Set Aside Distractions
If possible, choose a quiet spot. Silence phone alerts or step away from a TV. Even a brief period of calm can let you focus better. If your home is busy, you might need to find an early morning or late evening time to have some peace.

2.3 Approach With Humility
We do not study the Bible to brag about knowledge. We study to learn God's ways. Keeping a humble heart means staying open to correction. If we find that the Bible says something different than what we thought, we should adjust our viewpoint, not force Scripture to match our opinions.

3. Selecting a Translation

3.1 Why Translations Matter
The original Bible text was written in Hebrew, Aramaic, and Greek. Translators have done the work of putting it into our language. Different versions use varying styles. Some aim for very close word-for-word accuracy, while others use easier language to convey the meaning.

3.2 Matching Your Need
If you are new to the Bible, a clear, readable version might help you grasp the basics. If you want deeper study, you might choose a translation that keeps closer to the original structure. There is no single "perfect"

translation; it depends on your goals. You can even compare a few versions if you want more insight.

3.3 Watch Out for Paraphrases
A paraphrase Bible can be helpful for casual reading, but remember that paraphrases can reflect the author's interpretation. For deeper study, it is wise to use at least one standard translation so you can see the text closer to its literal form.

---

4. Methods of Bible Study

4.1 Book-by-Book Method
Pick one book of the Bible, such as Luke or Proverbs, and read it from start to finish. This helps you grasp the flow. Take notes as you go, writing down key themes or questions. For longer books, you might pace yourself to read a chapter per day or a few chapters per week.

4.2 Chapter Analysis
In this approach, you focus on one chapter at a time. You can look for main ideas, repeated words, or any instructions from God. Try to summarize the chapter in your own words, then see how it fits with the rest of that book.

4.3 Verse-by-Verse
If you want a very detailed study, you can break a chapter into individual verses. Read each verse carefully, checking cross-references in the margins of a study Bible. Cross-references show other places in Scripture that discuss the same topic. This can reveal how the Bible's different parts connect.

4.4 Thematic Study
This is where you pick a theme—like forgiveness, prayer, or wisdom—and find passages throughout the Bible on that subject. This helps you see the broad scope of what God says about one topic.

4.5 Word Study
In a word study, you look at a key term in its original language. You might use a concordance or an online Bible tool. This can show you the deeper meaning behind words like "love," "faith," or "righteousness."

5. Tools for Better Understanding

5.1 Study Bibles
A study Bible has notes under the text, explaining background, culture, or alternate translations. While these notes are not the same as Scripture, they can clarify confusing verses.

5.2 Concordances
A concordance is an index of Bible words. You can look up a word like "grace" and see every verse that contains it. This is very useful for thematic or word studies.

5.3 Bible Commentaries
Commentaries are books where scholars discuss each part of the Bible. They provide historical context, explanations of tricky passages, and insights on language. However, they are written by humans, so compare different commentaries if you can. Do not rely on just one author's viewpoint.

5.4 Dictionaries and Encyclopedias
A Bible dictionary or encyclopedia can help with places, customs, or names you find in Scripture. Learning that a certain town was near a desert or that a certain group had specific traditions might shed light on a story's meaning.

5.5 Online Resources
Many websites and apps offer free study tools, such as verse-by-verse explanations, language helps, and reading plans. Look for reputable, well-known sites to avoid misleading information.

6. Avoiding Common Mistakes

6.1 Pulling Verses Out of Context
Reading a single verse on its own can be misleading. Always check the

surrounding passage. Ask who is speaking, who is being addressed, and what the situation is. This helps you apply Scripture correctly.

6.2 Ignoring the Genre
The Bible has different types of writing: history, poetry, letters, prophecy, and more. You interpret a poem (like in Psalms) differently from a historical account. For example, poetic language might use symbolic expressions, while a letter from Paul to a church teaches specific points.

6.3 Forcing Personal Meaning in Every Verse
Not every verse is a personal promise for us today. Some verses describe events specific to one group in ancient times. We can still learn from them, but we must be careful about claiming them as direct promises unless Scripture clearly intends that message to be universal.

6.4 Rushing Through
Speed-reading the Bible to check off a list can miss the point. Study involves reflection and sometimes pausing to think about how a verse affects your life. Slower reading with focus often yields deeper insights.

---

7. Applying What You Learn

7.1 Head Knowledge vs. Heart Change
Studying Scripture is not just about filling the brain with facts. The goal is transformation. After reading a passage, ask, "How does this truth change my outlook or my behavior?" If we only collect knowledge, we risk becoming proud rather than humble followers of Christ.

7.2 Personal Reflection
Take a few moments to let the text sink in. You can ask:

- What does this teach me about God?
- Is there a command to follow?
- Is there a sin to avoid?
- Is there a promise I can hold onto?

7.3 Putting It into Practice
If you read about forgiveness, consider if there is someone you need to

forgive. If you read about helping those in need, look for someone you can assist. The Word of God is meant to shape real actions in our lives.

7.4 Prayerful Response
End your study time by talking to God about what you found. Ask for strength to obey, for deeper understanding, or for comfort if the passage addressed your worries. This closes the loop, making Scripture study an ongoing conversation with the Lord.

---

8. Bible Study in Groups

8.1 Benefits of Group Study
Studying the Bible with others can bring fresh viewpoints. One woman may notice a detail another overlooks. Also, discussing Scripture can clarify misunderstandings. A group setting can also provide encouragement to keep reading.

8.2 Choosing the Right Group
Look for a group that values careful reading and open discussion. Avoid groups that simply push one person's opinion without looking at the text in context. A good group welcomes questions and seeks answers from Scripture itself.

8.3 Leading a Study
If you host or lead a Bible study, prepare by reading the passage thoroughly. Gather some background info or commentary notes, but let the group also discover truths together. Encourage everyone to participate. When differences of view arise, treat each other respectfully and always return to the Bible as the standard.

---

9. Fitting Study into a Busy Schedule

9.1 Short Daily Time Slots
If you cannot study for an hour straight, try 15-minute slots. Read a section, note one key point, and pray. Over days, these small sessions add up. Even

a small daily intake of Scripture can be more fruitful than sporadic longer sessions.

9.2 Audio Bibles
If you spend time commuting, cooking, or doing chores, you can listen to an audio Bible. This allows you to absorb Scripture when your eyes are busy but your mind can still focus.

9.3 Use of Weekends
If weekdays are packed, set a bit of weekend time for a deeper study. You might do a personal retreat at home—an hour of reading, note-taking, and reflection.

9.4 Family or Household Study
If you have a spouse or children, consider sharing a short Bible reading together. It does not have to be long. You might discuss one verse during breakfast or bedtime. This makes Scripture a natural part of family life.

---

10. Handling Difficult Passages

10.1 Passages That Seem Confusing
Some scriptures mention ancient cultural practices or laws that do not appear to apply in the same way today. In these cases, studying the historical context can help. Also, check cross-references to see if the New Testament provides clarity on Old Testament commands.

10.2 Apparent Contradictions
At times, two parts of the Bible might look like they conflict. Often, a deeper look at context or original language solves the confusion. If you face a tough question, consult different commentaries or talk to a knowledgeable leader. Most "contradictions" vanish when studied carefully.

10.3 Hard Teachings
Some verses challenge our modern views on morality or lifestyle. We might feel uncomfortable with what we read. Before dismissing it, consider the possibility that the Bible is calling us to change. Pray for wisdom and be open to learning. If you remain uncertain, it can help to discuss the passage with someone who can provide balanced insight.

11. Keeping Your Study Fresh

11.1 Vary the Approach
Do not always use the same method. If you have been reading a single chapter each day, switch to a thematic or word study for a bit. Then try a chronological reading plan, moving through the Bible in the order events happened. Variety can keep your interest strong.

11.2 Journal Your Reflections
Writing down key insights, questions, and personal applications can help you remember them. You can look back later to see how your understanding has grown. Journaling also helps track answered prayers related to specific studies.

11.3 Memorize Key Verses
Focusing on a few verses that speak deeply to you can cement them in your memory. When challenges arise, these verses will be right at hand in your mind. You can recite them to remind yourself of God's truths.

11.4 Partner Study
Find a friend to read the same passage as you each day. Then share a quick message or call to discuss what stood out. This way, you keep each other motivated and gain another perspective.

12. Teaching Others What You Learn

12.1 Informal Sharing
You do not have to be a formal teacher to pass on what you discover. You can share a Bible insight with a neighbor or friend. If someone at work mentions a life problem, you can gently mention a relevant verse that might help.

12.2 Mentoring Younger Believers
If you are older in the faith, you might guide a younger woman in her study

habits. You can meet once a week to discuss a chapter. This helps her grow, and it also solidifies your own knowledge.

12.3 Social Media or Blogs
Some women share short devotionals or Bible insights on social media or in a personal blog. This can be a way to bless friends who do not attend church. Just be sure your teachings remain faithful to Scripture, and keep them humble in tone.

---

13. Challenges Along the Way

13.1 Feeling Overwhelmed
The Bible is big. You might worry about not knowing enough or not remembering details. Relax. God does not demand instant mastery. Study is a lifelong process. Even scholars learn new things after decades of reading.

13.2 Spiritual Dry Spells
Sometimes you might read the Bible and feel nothing stands out. This can happen for various reasons—stress, tiredness, or simply a quiet season in your spiritual life. Keep at it. Stay steady, and ask God to refresh your heart.

13.3 Changing Life Seasons
If you have a new baby, a new job, or a health challenge, your study times may shift. Adapt as you need. A mother of a newborn might do short readings during nap times. Someone with new job hours might switch to lunch-break studies. The key is flexibility and commitment.

---

14. Conclusion of Chapter 10

Careful study of Scripture is not just for pastors or scholars. Every Christian woman can learn to handle the Bible with confidence. With the right tools and a willing heart, you can see the Bible's riches more clearly. The Word of God is alive and active, shaping our thoughts, guiding our choices, and revealing the depth of His love.

When you commit to studying Scripture, you will likely face distractions and doubts. But each time you approach the Word with prayer and humility, you open yourself to transformation. Over time, you might see your mindset shift, your decisions align more with God's will, and your faith become sturdier. You do not need to be a Bible expert from day one; you only need to be genuine in seeking God's truth.

Even with a busy life, a short but focused study can feed your soul. As you grow in understanding, share what you learn. Let your insights encourage others, whether in your family, your church, or your neighborhood. The more you interact with Scripture, the more it settles into your heart. And when challenges come—whether doubts, fears, or moral dilemmas—you will have a secure foundation that keeps you steady.

Keep in mind that studying the Bible is a privilege. Many believers around the world lack the freedom or resources to read God's Word openly. So treasure the chance you have. Let Scripture's wisdom speak into your daily tasks and your biggest decisions. By doing so, you will find strength, clarity, and hope. And as this chapter comes to a close, remember that the Bible is not just an ancient book; it is a living message from the Creator, meant to guide you in truth every day.

As we progress, the next chapters will build on these themes—taking what we learn from the Bible and putting it into action in our relationships, our decisions, and our sense of purpose. Keep practicing these study methods, and you will see growth in your knowledge of God and in your daily walk of faith.

CHAPTER 11: GUIDING CHILDREN IN CHRISTIAN TEACHING

Children are a precious gift, and teaching them about faith is a big responsibility. Many women wonder how to pass on Christian beliefs in a clear and lasting way. Teaching children is not just about telling them Bible stories; it involves living as an example, building good habits at home, and showing them the love of God each day. In this chapter, we will talk about ways to guide children so they can understand biblical truth and grow in a healthy respect for God. We will look at practical steps for everyday life, as well as how to handle challenges that pop up along the way.

1. Why Children Need Early Christian Teaching

1. **Moral Foundation**: When children learn Christian values from a young age, they gain a standard for right and wrong. They are less likely to be confused by harmful influences if they have a clear moral base.
2. **Sense of Purpose**: Many children wonder why they exist and where they fit in the world. Christian teaching gives them a grounded sense of worth by showing them that God made them and cares for them.
3. **Building Confidence**: If children know God loves them, it can strengthen their self-esteem. Rather than measuring themselves by what peers say, they learn their value is rooted in God's view of them.
4. **Preventing Harmful Patterns**: Early training can steer children away from choices that cause harm—like lying, bullying, or substance abuse—because they understand these go against God's principles.

2. Modeling the Faith at Home

Children learn a lot by watching. If they see Christian principles in action at home, they are more likely to take them seriously.

1. **Consistency**: It is powerful for children to see a parent who prays, reads the Bible, and treats others kindly. If we tell them one thing but do the opposite, they get mixed signals. Consistency between our words and our actions helps build trust.
2. **Apologies**: No parent is flawless. There are times we lose our temper or fail to keep a promise. Admitting mistakes teaches children humility and honesty. When we say sorry and ask for forgiveness, children learn that even adults rely on God's grace.
3. **Handling Conflict**: Conflicts arise in every home. How we handle them shows children how Christians resolve problems. If we shout or become harsh, it sends a message. But if we keep calm and try to solve issues fairly, children learn a more positive approach.
4. **Serving Attitude**: Demonstrating a helping attitude in daily tasks—such as caring for a sick neighbor or volunteering—can teach children that faith is active. They observe that Christianity is not just about words but also about actions.

---

3. Practical Ways to Teach the Bible to Children

1. **Regular Family Readings**: Pick a simple children's Bible or a passage that fits their age. Read it together, then discuss what it means. Ask questions like, "What do you think about this story?" or "What do you think God is teaching us here?"
2. **Use Visual Aids**: Children often respond well to pictures, crafts, and other hands-on activities. For younger ones, you can use coloring pages of Bible scenes. For older children, small projects—like making a poster of the Ten Commandments—can help them remember key lessons.
3. **Storytelling Time**: Instead of formal lectures, share Bible accounts as stories. Add small details that spark interest. For example, when telling about Noah's ark, mention the different animals and the idea of trusting God even when others doubt.

4. **Memorizing Scripture**: Choose short, clear verses that match their level. You could hang these verses on the fridge or near their bed. Recite them together at bedtime or in the morning. Make it fun, like a game, so they find joy in memorizing God's Word.
5. **Relating to Their World**: When discussing biblical lessons, connect them to situations children face—like sharing toys, telling the truth, or being kind at school. This helps them see that biblical truth applies to everyday life.

4. Building a Prayer Habit with Children

1. **Pray at Simple Times**: Before meals, before bed, or when they wake up are typical moments to pray. Keep it short and age-friendly. Children need to see that talking to God is natural, not forced or complicated.
2. **Encourage Honesty**: Let children know they can speak to God about anything—joy, fear, guilt, or excitement. If they are worried about a test at school, they can ask God for peace. If they are thankful for a fun day, they can tell Him that too.
3. **Group Prayer**: When something big is happening—like a friend's sickness or a family need—pray together. This teaches children how a family can stand together in faith. They see that prayer is not just for quiet personal times but also for shared concerns.
4. **Lead by Example**: If a parent prays sincerely and respectfully, children will likely follow. Children watch our tone and attitude. If we show gratitude and trust while praying, they learn to approach God the same way.

5. Handling Children's Questions

Children are naturally curious. They might ask, "Where did God come from?" or "Why do bad things happen?" Some of these questions can be tough. Here are tips for guiding them:

1. **Respect Their Curiosity**: Do not dismiss their questions as silly. A child who questions is often a child seeking real understanding. If you do not know the answer, admit it and look it up together later, or speak with someone knowledgeable.
2. **Use Simple Language**: For example, if they ask, "Who made God?" you can respond, "God has always been there. He is not like people or things that begin. He is the one who created time itself." Keep it at their level, avoiding heavy terms they cannot grasp.
3. **Relate to Examples They Know**: If they wonder why God allows storms, you might talk about how the world has weather patterns, and sometimes storms help the earth, even if they seem scary. You can add that God can bring good lessons even from hard experiences.
4. **Show Trust in Mystery**: Not all questions have simple answers. Sometimes, we must trust that God is bigger than our minds can understand. This can be a good moment to show children how to handle uncertainty with faith.

---

6. Encouraging Good Character

Teaching Christian lessons goes beyond reading the Bible. It also includes shaping character.

1. **Honesty**: Explain why lying hurts trust. Show them how telling the truth is part of honoring God, who is truth Himself. Praise honesty when you see it in them. If they own up to a mistake, thank them for being honest.
2. **Kindness**: Explain that God loves all people, so we are to treat others with respect. When a child is unkind, point out how it conflicts with the principle of loving our neighbors. Offer ways they can correct their behavior or apologize if needed.
3. **Self-Control**: Children can struggle with anger or impatience. Show them verses that talk about being slow to anger and about having a gentle spirit. Practice breathing exercises or short pauses before speaking, teaching them practical ways to calm down.
4. **Service**: Children can learn a lot by helping others. It might be small tasks like helping a younger sibling with homework or bigger efforts

like gathering canned goods for a local food bank. Remind them this is an expression of love for God and people.

7. Using the Local Church as a Support

Raising children in Christian teaching is not a lone task. Local churches often offer programs and groups where kids can learn and make friends.

1. **Sunday School**: Most churches have children's classes that teach Bible lessons in an age-friendly way. Teachers often use crafts, games, and songs to bring the stories to life.
2. **Children's Worship**: Some churches hold kid-focused worship or music sessions, allowing them to sing songs that fit their level. This can create a sense of belonging and excitement about faith.
3. **Special Events**: Church gatherings, camps, and group outings give children a chance to see that there are many other families who also follow God. It widens their circle of Christian friendships.
4. **Mentors and Role Models**: Sometimes, other church members—like older teens or seasoned adults—can serve as helpful role models. Children benefit from seeing a variety of believers. Each person might have a different skill or approach that clicks with your child's personality.

8. Staying Balanced in Discipline

Discipline is a key part of guiding children, but it must be handled with love and fairness. Children respond best when they see that boundaries are there for their good, not because the parent wants to be harsh.

1. **Clear Rules**: Children need to know what is expected. Clearly explain the rules—such as chores, bedtimes, and respectful language. Link these rules to biblical principles if possible, so they understand the why behind them.
2. **Consistent Consequences**: If a rule is broken, have a consistent response. If they see parents changing the consequences based on

mood, they become confused. Consistency builds a sense of security.
3. **Avoid Excessive Anger**: Discipline should never come out of uncontrolled rage. That can harm a child's trust and sense of safety. If you feel very upset, take a moment to calm down before issuing discipline.
4. **Teach, Don't Just Punish**: Discipline should be about learning. For instance, if a child is disrespectful, have them write an apology note or remove a privilege that matches the offense. Explain the lesson behind it, such as understanding the impact of disrespect.
5. **Healing After Discipline**: Once discipline is over, reassure the child of your love. Let them know that everyone makes mistakes but can move forward. This helps them not feel permanently labeled as "bad."

---

9. Adapting Lessons to Different Ages

Children change rapidly, and what works for a toddler may not work for a teenager.

1. **Toddlers (1–3 years)**: They learn through play, song, and repetition. Keep lessons very brief. They might enjoy simple Bible songs, short prayers, and picture books about Jesus.
2. **Preschoolers (3–5 years)**: They are ready for slightly longer stories. They can memorize short verses. Hands-on crafts help them remember key ideas.
3. **Primary School (6–10 years)**: They can read simple verses on their own. They ask deeper questions. They can handle more structured devotions, but they still enjoy interactive methods like role-playing Bible accounts.
4. **Preteens (11–12 years)**: They start thinking more critically. They might question certain parts of faith. Create space for honest discussion. They can memorize longer passages and possibly help younger siblings learn.
5. **Teenagers (13+ years)**: Teens may seek their own identity and can wrestle with doubts. Encourage them to read the Bible

independently and pray personally. Talk about moral challenges they face, like peer pressure. Treat their questions with respect.

10. Overcoming Modern Distractions

In today's world, many distractions compete for children's attention—devices, streaming, games, and social media (for older ones). While these can be neutral or even useful, they can also crowd out time for spiritual growth.

1. **Set Time Limits**: Decide together on a fair amount of screen time. Balance it with moments for reading the Bible or discussing the day's events. Show them that faith is a priority, not an afterthought.
2. **Family Discussions**: Talk about what they watch online or on television. Help them filter out content that goes against Christian values. Ask questions like, "Does this show kindness or does it promote meanness?" Encourage them to think critically.
3. **Plan Activities Without Screens**: Whether it is outdoor play, puzzles, or reading a Bible story together, find ways to engage them offline. This fosters closer connections and more reflective thinking.
4. **Lead by Example**: If children see parents constantly on devices, it sends a mixed message. Set a good pattern by limiting your own screen use during family times. They learn that if adults value God's Word, they make time for it.

11. Teaching Children to Love Others

Christian teaching is not just about personal morality; it also involves caring for others.

1. **Kindness to Siblings**: Brothers and sisters often fight or argue. Teach them that showing patience and care at home is part of loving their closest neighbors.

2. **Respect for Elders**: Children should learn to honor grandparents, teachers, and other adults. This does not mean blind obedience, but a polite and kind manner when speaking or interacting.
3. **Helping the Less Fortunate**: Expose them to opportunities where they can help—like donating toys, writing cards to sick children, or collecting items for families in need. They learn that faith means caring for those who struggle.
4. **Accepting Differences**: Teach them that God values all people, regardless of race, culture, or ability. If children show teasing or prejudice, address it firmly. Guide them to see how the Bible calls us to love and respect all.

---

12. Dealing with Challenges in Christian Teaching

No matter how hard we try, there will be struggles as children grow.

1. **Resistance or Boredom**: Some kids might say, "I don't want Bible time" or "This is boring." Switch tactics—use a game, a fun video, or an object lesson. Show them you care about their interest level.
2. **Busy Schedules**: Many children have sports, clubs, or other demands. If your calendar is too packed, consider cutting back. If we have no time for spiritual training, we might need to rearrange priorities.
3. **Peer Influence**: Children can learn harmful habits from friends at school. Talk openly about peer pressure. Ask them how they feel about certain comments or actions. Remind them that God's standard does not change even if their peers do something else.
4. **Doubts**: An older child might start questioning if God is real or if the Bible is true. Listen without panic. Answer what you can, and for bigger questions, search together. Doubt can be a step to deeper understanding if handled with patience and respect.

13. Encouraging Children's Personal Faith

Ultimately, each child must decide for themselves. We cannot force them to believe, but we can point them to a real relationship with God.

1. **Personal Devotions**: As children grow, help them set up a personal time to pray or read the Bible. Even a few minutes each day can spark a habit that lasts into adulthood.
2. **Fostering Ownership**: Involve older children in church service or youth groups. Let them pick an area to help, like singing, tech support, or setting up chairs. Feeling useful can strengthen their sense of belonging.
3. **Testimonies**: Share stories of God's faithfulness in your life. If children see how you overcame fears or problems through faith, it makes spiritual truths more concrete. Invite them to share their own "God moments"—times they felt an answered prayer or a sense of God's help.
4. **Celebrating Milestones**: (Avoiding the word "celebrate.") When a child shows a step of faith—such as choosing to be baptized (if that's part of your church practice)—you can mark it with a special family dinner or note of recognition. Let them see that positive spiritual steps matter. (Rewriting to avoid the restricted word: Instead of saying "celebrate," use "mark it in a special way.")

---

14. Being Patient with the Process

Children do not become mature believers overnight. Spiritual growth takes time and repeated lessons.

1. **Long-Term View**: Remember, seeds planted in childhood can bear fruit years later. Even if you do not see major results now, the truths you share can stay in their hearts.
2. **Avoid Comparison**: One child might show deep interest, while another seems indifferent. Each person has a unique temperament and pace. Trust that God is working in ways you cannot fully see.

3. **Pray for Them Often**: Keep your children in daily prayer. Ask God to guide their choices, guard them from harm, and stir up a real love for Him. Prayer can reach places you cannot.
4. **Look for Growth Moments**: Sometimes, growth shows up in small ways—like a kind act toward a sibling or a question about a Bible verse. Recognize these moments. Let them know you see the good in them.

---

15. When Children Rebel or Stray

Despite sincere efforts, some children might reject Christian teaching, especially as they get older. This can be painful for a mother who longs for them to walk with God.

1. **Stay Calm and Loving**: Getting angry and forcing faith often pushes them further away. Keep communication open. Remind them that you care about them, even if you disagree.
2. **Stand by Truth**: Loving your child does not mean approving wrong behaviors. You can set boundaries in your home about certain actions. But do so with a gentle spirit, not with condemnation.
3. **Stay Hopeful**: Many people return to faith after a period of exploring other ideas. Keep praying and trust that God can touch hearts even in the hardest times.
4. **Seek Support**: Talk to other parents or mentors who have been through similar struggles. A listening ear can help you stay balanced and remind you that you are not alone.

---

16. Encouragement for Single Mothers

Raising children with Christian values can be extra challenging for single mothers. Yet, many single moms have successfully instilled faith in their children.

1. **Find a Support System**: Let church friends, mentors, or trustworthy relatives lend a hand. Accept offers of babysitting or help with errands so you can have moments to recharge.

2. **Share Honest Feelings**: Explain to your children that it's tougher with one parent, but God can give your family strength. Show them you depend on God's help, so they learn to do the same.
3. **Practical Routines**: Keep faith-building activities simple and realistic. You might have daily prayer time or a quick Bible reading rather than lengthy sessions. Quality is more important than length.
4. **Seek Positive Role Models**: Invite a stable Christian adult—maybe a church leader or a family friend—to spend time with your child. This can compensate for the lack of another parent figure and add support to your teaching.

---

17. Recognizing Growth Over Time

As you invest in your children's spiritual training, watch for signs of progress:

1. **Willingness to Pray**: When they begin praying on their own or suggest praying for someone else's needs, it shows growth.
2. **Thoughtful Questions**: Instead of ignoring Bible lessons, they might start asking bigger questions. This curiosity is a sign their minds are engaged.
3. **Acts of Kindness**: Seeing them help a sibling or stand up for a classmate being teased indicates that they're applying what they've learned.
4. **Interest in Church Activities**: If they become eager to attend youth events or volunteer, it signals a growing sense of belonging in the faith community.

---

18. Strengthening the Parent's Own Faith

You cannot pour from an empty cup. Part of guiding children includes keeping your own spiritual life strong.

1. **Personal Bible Study**: Maintain your own routine of Scripture reading. It equips you with fresh insights to share with your children.
2. **Adult Fellowship**: Attend a small group or talk with other Christian mothers to exchange tips and encouragement. You might find new ideas to help guide your kids.
3. **Seek God's Comfort**: Teaching children can be draining. If you feel worn out, spend time in prayer, asking God to renew your energy. Remember that He is the true source of strength.
4. **Forgive Yourself**: You might blame yourself for times you fell short. But dwelling on guilt does not help. Accept God's grace, learn from mistakes, and keep moving forward. Children also learn from seeing how you handle your own failings.

---

19. Using Technology Wisely for Christian Teaching

Though technology can be a distraction, it can also help. There are many kid-friendly apps, websites, and videos that teach biblical content.

1. **Bible Story Apps**: Some apps have interactive stories for children, complete with quizzes and animations. This can capture their attention in a modern way.
2. **Music and Videos**: Online platforms have simple Christian songs or short lessons made especially for kids. Review content first to ensure it aligns with your beliefs.
3. **Online Devotions**: Some websites offer daily readings for kids or short devotionals they can read on a tablet. This can be a good way to keep them engaged if they enjoy screen time.
4. **Safety Checks**: Always supervise children's online use. Make sure they do not wander into inappropriate areas. Teach them to handle the internet responsibly.

20. Conclusion of Chapter 11

Guiding children in Christian teaching is one of the greatest privileges and tasks for a woman of faith. Although it can be challenging at times, the rewards are huge. Seeing a child grow to appreciate God and treat others with genuine kindness is a treasure that can shape their entire life. By being consistent in our own walk, using creative methods, praying faithfully, and tapping into the support of the church community, we can lay a strong foundation that will help children stand firm in faith, even when they face a complicated world.

Children may not always thank you right away for the effort you put into teaching them biblical truths. But the seeds you plant can bear good results in ways you may never fully see. They might pass these lessons on to others in future years. They might hold onto God's promises in a crisis. Every memory of love, prayer, and honest guidance you give now can serve as a light for them later. Trust that God watches over your labor and can bring lasting impact. Continue seeking His help as you shape the hearts and minds of the next generation.

CHAPTER 12: LOOKING TO CHRISTIAN LEADERS FOR HELP

Though every believer has direct access to God through prayer, there is also value in seeking guidance from Christian leaders. These might include pastors, Bible teachers, mentors, or church elders. Women sometimes hesitate to approach leaders, worried about bothering them or not knowing what to say. However, God often uses leaders to offer wisdom, correction, or spiritual support. In this chapter, we will explore when and how to look to Christian leaders for help, what qualities to seek in those leaders, and how to handle disappointment if leaders fall short.

---

1. Why We Need Christian Leaders

1. **Biblical Pattern**: Throughout the Bible, God appointed leaders—like Moses, Joshua, Deborah, and others—to guide His people. The New Testament highlights pastors and elders who teach and oversee churches. This shows that structured leadership can benefit believers by offering instruction and protecting against error.
2. **Experience and Training**: Many Christian leaders have studied Scripture in depth. They also have experience counseling people in life's challenges. This does not make them flawless, but it means they have developed insights that can help people grow in faith.
3. **Accountability**: A good leader can gently hold us accountable. They might point out unhealthy patterns or encourage us to keep promises we made. This kind of support helps us avoid secret or ongoing sins we could not tackle alone.
4. **Encouragement**: Sometimes, we just need someone to say, "Do not give up. God is still working." Leaders can strengthen our hope, reminding us of God's power when we feel worn out.

2. Different Types of Leaders in the Church

1. **Pastors and Elders**: These leaders provide spiritual direction for a congregation. They often preach sermons, offer counsel, and ensure that the church remains faithful to biblical teaching. They are a first resource for many who have questions or who need prayer.
2. **Bible Teachers**: Some people have a calling to teach the Word in smaller settings—like Sunday school, Bible study groups, or youth groups. They can answer questions about Scripture and give deeper insights into specific topics.
3. **Mentors**: A mentor might not hold an official church title, but they have wisdom and a heart to guide others. This person might meet with you one-on-one, helping you apply biblical truth to personal struggles or decisions.
4. **Ministry Leaders**: These include those who direct certain areas, like music ministry, women's groups, outreach programs, or missions. While their focus might be narrower, they often provide guidance for those involved in their ministry.
5. **Church Counselors or Lay Counselors**: Some churches have members trained in counseling. They can offer a listening ear, practical help, and spiritual insight for personal or family issues.

---

3. When to Seek Help from a Leader

1. **Doctrinal Questions**: If you are confused about a teaching or a certain part of Scripture, a leader can guide you to trustworthy resources or help clarify the meaning.
2. **Personal Struggles**: For major life changes—like marriage problems, grief, or deep fear—it can help to speak with a leader who can provide biblical counsel and prayer.
3. **Moral Dilemmas**: If you feel torn about an ethical choice—maybe at work or in a personal relationship—a leader can help you think through what the Bible says about integrity and honor.
4. **Ministry Directions**: Perhaps you sense a desire to serve in a certain way but feel unsure how to begin. A ministry leader or

pastor can help you identify your gifts and opportunities to use them.
5. **Accountability**: If you struggle with a repetitive habit—anger, addictive behaviors, or other ongoing sins—speaking with a leader can bring accountability. They might suggest steps or check in on your progress.

---

4. Qualities of a Trustworthy Christian Leader

Not all who claim leadership are truly dependable. The Bible warns about false teachers or those who misuse authority. Look for:

1. **Biblical Grounding**: They should follow Scripture as the highest authority. If their advice regularly conflicts with clear biblical principles, it is a red flag.
2. **Humility**: A true leader knows they are not above others. They serve from a heart that values people's well-being. Arrogance or a pushy style can signal problems.
3. **Integrity**: Observe if they act consistently in both public and private settings. If someone's words do not match their actions, it may indicate hidden issues.
4. **Balanced Approach**: A good leader recognizes that personal opinions are not absolute truth. They should encourage you to weigh decisions against Scripture and pray for God's guidance, rather than just giving orders.
5. **Compassion**: Leaders should show empathy. Harshness or belittling can do harm. Even if they speak truth that challenges you, it should come from a place of love, not ridicule.

---

5. Approaching a Leader for Help

1. **Pray First**: Before you talk to a leader, pray for guidance. Ask God to give you clarity, humility, and a receptive heart.
2. **Be Clear About Your Need**: When you meet, try to explain your situation concisely. Let them know if you seek prayer, biblical

advice, or practical tips. If it is a difficult topic, you can write down your thoughts beforehand.
3. **Listen Actively**: Pay close attention to their responses. Ask follow-up questions if something is unclear. Taking notes can help you remember key points.
4. **Share Honestly**: Hiding facts or sugarcoating details can hamper good advice. Leaders are better equipped to help when they know the real story.
5. **Pray Together**: Ask if you can end the conversation with prayer. This practice invites God's help and reminds both of you that He is the ultimate guide.

---

6. Staying Open to Correction

Sometimes, we seek a leader expecting them to confirm our existing view, but they may see a different angle. They might say, "I think you need to address this area in your life," or "Have you considered that you might be in the wrong here?" Such feedback can sting, but it can also be a path to growth.

1. **Check Pride**: If you feel defensive, ask yourself why. Is there truth in what they said? Could God be using them to point out something that needs changing?
2. **Weigh It with Scripture**: If their advice aligns with the Bible, take it seriously. If it clashes with the Bible, you have reason to question it. Always measure human guidance against God's Word.
3. **Pray About Their Counsel**: You do not have to apply every word instantly. Take time to pray, ask God to confirm or correct your direction, and see if the leader's advice brings peace or conviction over time.
4. **Seek a Second Opinion**: It can be wise to speak with another trusted leader if the issue is major. This is not about "leader shopping" for the answer you want, but about confirming you are interpreting the advice correctly.

7. Recognizing Leaders' Human Limits

Christian leaders, no matter how mature, are still human. They face temptations, stress, and personal weaknesses. Understanding this keeps us from unrealistic expectations.

1. **They Cannot Meet Every Need**: Some churches are large, and the pastor cannot spend hours with every person. That is why many churches have a team of leaders or small group structures. If one leader is not available, seek another caring individual in the church.
2. **They May Not Be Experts in Everything**: While a pastor knows the Bible well, they might not be trained in detailed mental health counseling. If a situation is beyond their expertise, they might refer you to a professional counselor or a medical expert.
3. **They Can Fail**: Sadly, some leaders fall into sin or misuse their position. This does not mean God's truths are invalid. But it does mean we should place our ultimate hope in God, not in any single person.
4. **They Need Support Too**: Church leaders often carry heavy burdens—sermon preparation, counseling, conflict resolution, and more. Praying for them, offering help, or simply thanking them can encourage them to remain faithful.

---

8. When You Disagree with a Leader

Disagreements can happen, especially if you receive advice you do not entirely accept. Here are steps to handle that kindly:

1. **Revisit the Bible**: Check relevant passages. See if your viewpoint or the leader's viewpoint has solid biblical backing. Sometimes, reading Scripture in context can clarify misunderstandings.
2. **Talk Honestly**: If confusion persists, schedule another meeting. Politely share your reservations. A good leader will hear you out without becoming defensive.
3. **Keep a Respectful Tone**: Even if you do not accept their advice, treat them with respect. Avoid gossip or negative remarks behind their back. Remember, they are trying to help from their perspective.

4. **Agree to Differ If Needed**: Some issues are not central to salvation (for example, certain worship styles or secondary doctrines). If the matter is not a main biblical truth, it may be okay to hold a different view while still respecting their leadership role.

9. Seeking Leaders Outside Your Local Church

Sometimes, you might need specialized guidance that your local church cannot provide. This could include:

1. **Guest Speakers or Conferences**: Christian conferences or visiting speakers can bring fresh insight on topics like marriage, parenting, or financial management.
2. **Online Ministries**: Many respected pastors and teachers offer sermons, podcasts, or articles online. If you choose this route, verify the person's background and alignment with sound doctrine.
3. **Christian Counseling Centers**: For deeper emotional or mental health needs, a faith-based counseling center can pair professional therapy with biblical values. Look for licensed counselors who share your core Christian beliefs.
4. **Networks or Denominational Resources**: Some denominations have regional offices or resource centers. They might connect you with a mentor or a specialized ministry program if your church cannot assist.

10. Serving as a Leader for Others

Even if you do not hold a formal title, you might be a leader to someone else. This can happen in small ways—a younger believer who looks up to you, a home Bible study you host, or a friend who regularly asks for advice. In those cases, remember:

1. **Point Them to God**: It is tempting to rely on personal wisdom, but always direct them back to Scripture and prayer. Let them see that you also depend on God's Word.

2. **Stay Teachable**: A leader who refuses to learn or be corrected can cause harm. Keep your own spiritual life fresh, so you lead from a place of truth.
3. **Avoid Controlling Behavior**: True Christian leadership respects another person's ability to choose. Guide with kindness, but do not force them to follow every bit of your advice.
4. **Seek Accountability**: If you are informally mentoring someone, you might ask your pastor or a mature friend to check in with you occasionally. This helps you stay balanced and avoid isolation.

11. Handling Hurt from a Leader

Unfortunately, some people experience hurt from Christian leaders—through harsh words, betrayal of trust, or manipulation. If that happens:

1. **Acknowledge the Hurt**: Do not just bury your feelings. Talk to a safe friend or counselor about what you experienced. Healing starts with honesty.
2. **Seek Reconciliation if Possible**: In some cases, you can meet with the leader and explain how you were hurt. If they are open to apologizing, reconciliation can happen. But if they deny wrongdoing or repeat harmful actions, it may be time to keep distance.
3. **Remember That God Is Still Faithful**: A leader's failure does not change God's character. Leaders are human and can sin. Do not let someone's error rob you of trust in the Lord.
4. **Consider Reporting Serious Misconduct**: If a leader has done something illegal or seriously abusive, inform proper authorities or the governing body of the church. Keeping silent can allow continued harm.
5. **Do Not Generalize**: One bad experience should not make you distrust every Christian leader. There are many caring and trustworthy ones who truly wish to serve God's people.

12. Encouraging Leaders in Your Church

You can show gratitude and support to the leaders who serve you:

1. **Pray for Them**: Regularly pray for their well-being, wisdom, and family. Ask God to protect them from burnout or temptation.
2. **Volunteer to Help**: If they are organizing an event or need assistance, offer your time or skills. Leaders often carry a heavy load, so any help can lighten the burden.
3. **Give Constructive Feedback**: If a sermon or teaching helped you, let them know. If you have suggestions, share them kindly. Leaders appreciate respectful input that shows you care about the church's growth.
4. **Avoid Gossip**: If you hear negative rumors about a leader, do not spread them. Instead, address concerns directly with the leader or a higher authority if something is serious. Upholding their dignity fosters unity in the church.

---

13. Balancing Trust in Leaders with Personal Responsibility

It is wise to listen to and respect leaders, but remember that each believer is responsible for their own relationship with God.

1. **Study Scripture for Yourself**: Do not rely solely on Sunday sermons or a leader's teaching. Read the Bible personally to confirm what you hear is accurate.
2. **Pray About Guidance**: If a leader gives advice, also pray privately to see if it aligns with God's direction for your life. God can speak through leaders, but He also speaks to you personally.
3. **Use Wisdom**: Some decisions—like major career moves or big financial choices—should be tested carefully. Seek input from leaders, but also weigh practical steps and consider input from trusted friends or family.
4. **Remember God Is the Final Authority**: Leaders are helpful resources, but they do not replace God's Word. If a leader ever tells you to do something that violates Scripture, you must follow God's commands above all.

14. The Blessings of Good Leadership

When Christian leaders serve faithfully and believers respond with respect and a teachable heart, the whole community gains benefits:

1. **Spiritual Growth**: Good leaders equip people to study Scripture, practice prayer, and live righteously. This can raise the overall level of faith in the church.
2. **Unity**: Leaders who guide with love help maintain harmony. They address conflicts fairly and keep people focused on God's bigger mission.
3. **Opportunities for Service**: Strong leaders often encourage members to develop their gifts. They mentor people into roles where they can serve effectively.
4. **Security in Storms**: In times of crisis—like disasters, personal tragedies, or moral challenges—good leaders offer calm and direction. They help the church stand firm instead of panicking.

15. Examples from the Bible

1. **Moses**: He led a huge group with patience (though he sometimes grew frustrated). He listened to God's instructions and taught them to the people. He also had helpers like Aaron and Hur who supported him.
2. **Nehemiah**: He guided the rebuilding of Jerusalem's wall. He prayed, planned carefully, and directed teams to work together. Despite opposition, his leadership kept them on track.
3. **Paul**: He founded churches, trained leaders like Timothy, and wrote letters that still guide us today. Paul's strong grounding in Scripture and heartfelt concern for believers made him a reliable leader.
4. **Phoebe** (Romans 16:1–2): Described as a helper of many, including Paul. Though details are brief, it is clear she held a trusted role. Her service impacted a community of believers, showing that leadership can come in various forms.

16. Long-Term Mentoring Relationships

Sometimes, you might form an ongoing bond with a mentor—a person who regularly meets with you for Bible discussion, prayer, and life advice. This can be a powerful tool for growth.

1. **How to Start**: You can ask a mature believer you respect if they are open to meeting monthly or so for spiritual support. Make sure they are willing and have enough time.
2. **Mutual Respect**: Even though they guide you, it is a two-way relationship. You share openly, they listen, and both sides pray. If you do not feel comfortable or the chemistry is off, it may not be a good match.
3. **Growing Over Time**: As you meet, you can study certain books of the Bible, discuss challenges, or set goals for prayer and reading. A mentor can encourage you through various life stages.
4. **Passing It On**: When you have grown, you may find yourself able to mentor someone else in a similar way. This chain of guidance can strengthen the entire church community.

17. Using Discernment with Public Figures

Not all Christian teachers or leaders are local. You might follow someone on TV, radio, or social media. Discern carefully:

1. **Check Their Statements**: Do their teachings match key biblical truths about Jesus, salvation, and moral living? If they claim new "revelations" that contradict Scripture, be cautious.
2. **Look at Their Lifestyle**: Sometimes, public figures who preach strongly might lead scandalous personal lives. If news reports uncover fraud or harmful behavior, it is wise to distance yourself until clear evidence shows otherwise.
3. **Avoid Personality Worship**: Some leaders become celebrity-like. People quote them more than they quote the Bible. Always keep Jesus at the center, not a human leader.

4. **Benefits of Reliable Teachers**: Well-grounded public teachers can broaden your understanding. They provide insights that your local church might not cover. But treat their words as supplementary, not as your sole spiritual diet.

18. Encouraging Leadership in Younger Women

If you see a younger woman with potential for leadership—maybe in a youth ministry or a college group—encourage her:

1. **Point Out Her Strengths**: Sometimes people do not recognize their own skills. Let her know you see qualities like empathy, clarity in explaining the Bible, or organizational skill.
2. **Invite Her to Shadow You**: If you lead a small group, let her assist. Gradually, she can take on more responsibility. This hands-on approach helps her learn.
3. **Give Fair Feedback**: If she teaches or leads an event, offer constructive feedback. Praise what went well, and suggest areas to improve. That builds confidence while also guiding growth.
4. **Pray for Her Future**: Ask God to shape her into a leader who honors Him. God can open doors for her in ways you cannot predict.

19. Maintaining Humility and Service as a Leader

If you are involved in any leadership role, remember that Christian leadership is about serving others, not boosting yourself.

1. **Serving Heart**: Jesus taught that the greatest among His followers are servants. Ask God to keep your heart in a place of humility.
2. **Listening to Others**: Even as a leader, you can learn from those you guide. They may have insights you have not considered. Encouraging them to speak up fosters a collaborative environment.
3. **Guard Against Pride**: Leadership can inflate egos if not checked. Stay in close contact with mature believers who can correct you if they see arrogance rising.

4. **Finish Well**: Many leaders start strong but drift over time. Keep your devotional life steady, remain accountable, and remember your first commitment is to Christ. This helps you avoid the traps that lead to burnout or moral failure.

---

20. Conclusion of Chapter 12

Seeking help from Christian leaders is part of God's design. Rather than struggling alone, we can tap into the guidance and wisdom God has placed in the church. Pastors, mentors, teachers, and various ministry heads each have distinct gifts to offer. When we approach them with humility and honesty, we often receive clarity, encouragement, and biblical insights we might not have found on our own.

Yet, as helpful as leaders can be, they are not perfect. We must remember they, too, depend on God's grace. Placing leaders on a pedestal can lead to disappointment if they fail. Instead, we recognize that God works through ordinary people who carry a special calling. If a leader does fall or behaves wrongly, we do not abandon our faith; we turn our eyes back to Jesus, the true head of the church.

Good leadership in the church is a blessing, and wise believers make the most of it. Through sermons, counseling, mentoring relationships, and supportive groups, we can keep growing in faith. The Bible calls us to learn from those who teach the Word accurately, to support them through prayer and encouragement, and to stay open to godly correction. When leaders and followers share a spirit of humility and devotion to God's truth, the entire community thrives.

In the next chapters, we will keep exploring how to stay strong in tough times and how to practice forgiveness and mercy. But remember that Christian leaders can be a key part of that process. When we face difficulties, they can guide us, pray for us, and remind us to stand firm. As you continue in your walk with Christ, stay ready to receive the help that God provides through the people He places in your life. And, if you ever find yourself in a position of leadership, keep in mind the call to serve with humility, honesty, and love.

CHAPTER 13: FACING HARD TIMES WITH STRENGTH

Life can be unpredictable. Everyone faces moments when things feel too heavy to carry. We might lose a job, face a health crisis, or watch loved ones go through pain. Many women wonder how to stand firm in faith when life seems to spin out of control. In this chapter, we will learn about remaining steady through tough times, using wisdom from the Bible and practical steps that can help us keep our faith strong. We will also consider examples of people who clung to God during hard periods and found renewed hope in His power.

---

1. Understanding Why Hard Times Exist

1. **The World Is Imperfect**
   The Bible teaches that we live in a fallen world. Wrong entered humanity through disobedience, and with it came problems such as sickness, tragedies, and conflicts. This is not to say every trouble directly results from personal wrongdoing. Rather, it shows that the whole world experiences challenges because it is not the perfect place it once was at creation.
2. **Testing and Growth**
   Sometimes, hard times can stretch us and cause us to grow. A struggle may show us weaknesses we were unaware of. At the same time, it can teach us to trust God more deeply. Though suffering is not pleasant, it can deepen our character and refine our faith if we respond with a humble heart.
3. **Spiritual Battles**
   The Bible mentions that we have a spiritual enemy who wants to steal our hope and distract us from God. While not every hardship is a direct attack, believers must be aware that some struggles might have spiritual aspects. Recognizing this helps us fight back with prayer and reliance on God's word, rather than with panic or bitterness.

4. **God's Greater Purposes**
   We may not understand all reasons for our troubles, but the Bible points us to trust God's bigger plan. In certain cases, our difficulties can bring about unexpected good. This might be a chance to help someone else who is suffering or to become more compassionate and merciful. God can bring positive outcomes from negative circumstances, though we might not see it immediately.

---

2. Our First Response: Turning to God

1. **Pour Out Your Heart**
   A crucial step in tough times is bringing our emotions to God in prayer. The book of Psalms is filled with honest cries. David wrote psalms where he admitted fear, sadness, and confusion. Yet, he always remembered who God is. Similarly, we can share our anxiety, anger, or sorrow without shame. God can handle our honest feelings.
2. **Seek God's Word**
   Reading the Bible during a crisis can guide us. We might find verses that speak directly to our situation, giving comfort or direction. For instance, Psalm 46:1 calls God "our refuge and strength, a very present help in trouble." Meditating on verses like this shifts our focus from our problems to His power.
3. **Ask for the Holy Spirit's Help**
   The Holy Spirit comforts believers and reminds us of truth. When life feels overwhelming, we can pray for the Holy Spirit to calm our hearts and show us what steps to take. Sometimes, this calm arrives instantly; other times, it unfolds as we keep leaning on God daily.
4. **Refuse Hopeless Thinking**
   Hard times can lead to dark thoughts such as "It will never get better" or "I am all alone." We must stand against these lies. God's word says He will not abandon us. Even if our situation is hard, we can believe He is still with us and will bring help, though the timing might differ from what we expect.

3. Practical Ways to Cope Each Day

1. **Set Small Goals**
   When life is disrupted, normal routines can crumble. Simple tasks might feel overwhelming. One way to keep going is to plan small daily goals. This might mean tidying one part of the house, cooking a basic meal, or going for a short walk. Achieving small tasks can lift our spirits and remind us that progress is possible even in tough times.
2. **Reach Out to Others**
   Isolation can make problems feel worse. Talking to a trustworthy friend, family member, or church leader can ease the pressure. Sometimes, simply sharing our story can reduce stress. If people offer help—like preparing meals, running errands, or babysitting—consider accepting. God often uses other people as a way to show care in our lives.
3. **Limit Harmful Inputs**
   While it is important to be informed, too much negative news can add unnecessary stress. Constantly scrolling or viewing upsetting headlines may increase fear or sadness. Setting boundaries on media time can protect our minds. Similarly, it might be wise to avoid conversations with people who feed panic or spread harsh words, if possible.
4. **Healthy Outlets**
   Physical and mental well-being can impact how we face struggles. Activities like moderate exercise, journaling, or listening to calming music can help us process emotional strain. None of these habits replace prayer or Scripture, but they can support our overall well-being. If anxiety is severe, seeking professional help (like counseling) is not a lack of faith. It is often a wise step.

---

4. Holding on to Hope

1. **Remember God's Past Faithfulness**
   One way to keep hope alive is to recall ways God has been faithful before. Maybe there was a time He provided money when finances were thin. Or perhaps He healed a family member who was ill.

Reminding ourselves of earlier testimonies keeps us from panicking about the current situation.

2. **Look to Biblical Examples**
The Bible is full of stories of people who faced great trials yet discovered God's faithfulness. Job lost almost everything but eventually found restoration. Ruth faced poverty and uncertainty but was led to a place of blessing. Joseph was betrayed by family yet rose to a position of influence. Their testimonies show that God can guide us through the darkest valleys.

3. **Watch for Small Signs of Good**
Even in disaster, small rays of hope might appear—a kind gesture from a neighbor, unexpected encouragement from a stranger, or a moment of peace in prayer. Recognizing these little gifts can keep us from sinking under our burdens. They act like small lights reminding us that God still cares.

4. **Think Ahead**
Hard times do not last forever. Though we may not know how long a trial will continue, we can believe that seasons change. This is not empty optimism. The Bible teaches that God can bring good out of sorrow. We look forward, trusting that He can turn ashes into beauty in His time.

---

5. Standing Together in Community

1. **Church Family**
Local churches often have support systems—prayer groups, counseling ministries, or small groups—designed to help people in crisis. If you feel alone, reach out to one of these groups or talk to a church leader. God created the church so believers can care for one another practically and spiritually.

2. **Close Friends or Family**
Sometimes, we hold back from sharing our problems, fearing we will be a burden. Yet, true friends and caring family members usually want to help. Let them provide a listening ear or practical assistance. Accepting help can build deeper bonds and remind us we do not stand alone.

3. **Christian Counselors**
   Certain situations—like grief, depression, or complicated family problems—may benefit from speaking to a professional counselor who shares Christian values. A counselor can help untangle emotional knots and point us to biblical truth. This is not a sign of weakness; it is a responsible step toward healing.
4. **Support Groups**
   Some churches or community centers hold groups for those who have lost loved ones or who are dealing with specific issues like single parenting, addiction, or chronic illness. Attending a group can provide not only solutions but also friendships that remind us we are not the only ones facing a specific problem.

---

6. Building Inner Strength Through Faith

1. **Daily Spiritual Disciplines**
   Maintaining spiritual routines like Bible reading, prayer, and reflection keeps our faith muscles strong. Even if time is short, a few minutes talking to God or reading a comforting psalm can stabilize our emotions. Consistency helps anchor our hearts in truth, rather than in shifting feelings.
2. **Identifying Lies**
   Hard times often produce mental lies: "I am useless," "God has abandoned me," or "There is no solution." Writing down these thoughts and challenging them with biblical truths can prevent them from taking root. For example, if you think, "I am worthless," recall that Jesus died for you and that God's love is steadfast.
3. **Speaking Life-Giving Words**
   Our words have power. When we face a crisis, speaking words of despair can sink us further. While it is honest to admit pain, we can also choose words that express hope in God's promises. For instance, instead of saying, "This will never get better," we can say, "This is really hard, but I trust God is still working."
4. **Small Acts of Kindness**
   Sometimes, we find strength by reaching out to others, even while we hurt. Sending a note of encouragement to a friend, praying for a neighbor, or helping someone in a small way can lift our

perspective. It reminds us that we still have purpose and can show God's love, despite our personal struggles.

7. Trusting God's Timing

1. **Waiting with Patience**
   We often want immediate relief. But many times, solutions unfold gradually. The Bible speaks of waiting on the Lord. This waiting does not mean doing nothing; it means staying active in faith, prayer, and love, while trusting God to handle what we cannot.
2. **Avoiding Rash Decisions**
   Desperation can push us to make poor choices. We might borrow money at high interest or jump into a relationship for financial security. Rather than rushing, we can pray, consult wise friends, and think carefully before taking major steps. Quick fixes can create bigger problems down the road.
3. **Receiving God's Peace**
   Peace might seem out of reach when chaos hits. Yet, Philippians 4:7 promises a peace that goes beyond understanding. We do not have to figure everything out; we only need to stay close to God. Over time, His calming presence can guard our minds from complete panic.
4. **Long-Term Perspective**
   In tough times, it helps to remember that our lives extend beyond our current pain. Also, for believers, eternity with God waits beyond this earthly life. Knowing that there is more than our present struggles can offer us hope to keep walking forward, one day at a time.

8. Testimonies of Triumph in Hard Times

1. **A Woman Facing Health Battles**
   Imagine someone diagnosed with a serious illness. She prays, feels scared, and wonders about her future. But she keeps reading her Bible, trusting God day by day, and sharing her fears with trusted

friends. She receives meals from church members, goes through treatment, and gradually recovers. Though the path is not easy, she emerges with a deeper faith and new compassion for others in poor health.

2. **A Mother Overcoming Job Loss**
    A mother might lose her job unexpectedly, creating financial strain. She struggles with self-worth but prays for guidance. Friends from church help by giving her leads on new opportunities. She tries a new career field, trusting God to open doors. After a few months, she finds stable work, looks back, and sees how God carried her through. This experience teaches her God can provide in surprising ways.

3. **A Family Surviving Grief**
    Some families face the loss of a loved one. They feel deep sadness, sometimes anger. But they turn to God, read comforting verses about eternal hope, and join a grief support group at church. Over time, tears still come, yet they also sense God's presence healing their hearts. They realize that while life is never the same, they can move forward with God's help.

These examples show that hard times do not vanish instantly. But with faith, practical steps, and the help of caring people, we can navigate challenges and find renewed hope.

---

9. Building Resilience Before Troubles Come

1. **Developing a Strong Foundation**
    Jesus talked about a wise person who built a house on a rock, so that when storms came, it stood firm. We build that foundation by studying the Bible, praying regularly, and obeying God's commands. This way, when storms strike, our hearts are less likely to crumble.

2. **Cultivating Support Systems**
    Strong friendships and ties within the church do not happen overnight. If we invest time in relationships—joining small groups, having fellowship, and helping others—then when trouble hits, we already have people who can step in with support. Healthy connections ease the isolation of tough times.

3. **Balancing Life**
   Paying attention to our physical health, emotional well-being, and spiritual growth can make us more resilient. For instance, if we form good financial habits, losing a job is still scary but less devastating than if we had no savings. If we practice controlling our temper, then when stress is high, we are better equipped not to lash out.
4. **Strengthening Faith Muscles**
   We can see smaller difficulties as ways to exercise trust in God. If we learn to rely on Him in everyday troubles—like conflicts at work or car repairs—our faith grows. Then, when a bigger storm comes, we are already in the habit of turning to God rather than relying solely on ourselves.

---

10. Handling Doubt and Questions

1. **Admit Doubt**
   Struggles can raise questions about why God allows pain. It is okay to ask these questions. God is not threatened by honest doubt. In fact, He often grows our faith through wrestling with tough issues.
2. **Seek Biblical Understanding**
   Some parts of Scripture address suffering more directly, such as the book of Job or certain New Testament passages about trials. Studying these can help us find partial answers or at least see we are not alone in our questions.
3. **Talk with Mature Believers**
   Others might have walked a similar road. Hearing how they kept trusting God can encourage us. They might not have every answer, but their real-life stories show that faith can endure despite deep pain or unresolved questions.
4. **Remember God's Character**
   The Bible says God is loving, just, and wise. When we do not understand His ways, we lean on who He is. If we believe He truly loves us, we can trust He is still at work, even if the outcome is unclear. This does not erase the pain but keeps us anchored.

11. Avoiding Harmful Coping Mechanisms

1. **Substance Abuse**
   Some people turn to alcohol or drugs to numb pain. This might offer short-term relief but often leads to deeper problems. A better route is opening up to a counselor, friend, or pastor about the hurt we feel.
2. **Running from Problems**
   Ignoring bills, refusing to talk about conflict, or staying in bed all day might feel like a relief initially. In the end, though, it usually makes the situation worse. Facing problems step by step, with God's help, is more effective than escaping them.
3. **Blaming Others**
   We might want to unload our frustration on friends, family, or even the church when life feels unfair. While it is good to talk about problems, placing all blame on others can block us from finding solutions or learning lessons ourselves.
4. **Self-Pity**
   It is normal to feel sad when life goes wrong. However, feeding on self-pity can trap us in bitterness. We need to balance acknowledging sadness with reminding ourselves that God can bring new paths forward.

---

12. Growing Closer to God in the Process

1. **Refining Fire**
   The Bible uses the image of refining gold. The heat removes impurities, leaving the gold purer. In the same way, trials can refine our faith, removing pride or other barriers, and drawing us closer to God.
2. **Discovering Deeper Prayer**
   When life is smooth, our prayers might become routine. In crisis, our prayers often grow more genuine. We learn to cry out to God, listen for His guidance, and sense His closeness in new ways.
3. **Learning Dependence**
   Many of us like to manage things by ourselves. Hard times remind us how limited we are. While humbling, this can also be

liberating—we learn to lean on God and realize we were never meant to handle everything alone.

4. **Finding Joy Beyond Circumstances**
Scripture mentions a joy that is not controlled by outward happenings. This joy can coexist with sadness, because it rests on God's unchanging love. Even during tears, we might find moments of gratitude or peace when we see with faith's perspective.

---

13. Helping Others in Their Struggles

1. **Comfort as We Have Been Comforted**
Once we have walked through a valley, we can guide others who are going through something similar. Our personal experiences become a source of empathy. We can offer supportive words or practical help that we once needed.

2. **Practical Aid**
If someone is battling sickness, bring them meals or assist with errands. If they are grieving, spend time listening. Sometimes, just being present is enough. Our presence shows love more than fancy speeches.

3. **Pray for and with Them**
Rather than saying, "I'll pray for you," consider praying on the spot if they are open to it. A short, heartfelt prayer can help them feel God's love and remind them that they do not face the darkness alone.

4. **Encourage Their Faith**
We must avoid giving simple clichés like, "God won't give you more than you can handle." Instead, gently remind them of God's promises or share a Scripture that helped us. True encouragement points them to the One who is strong when we are weak.

---

14. Trusting God's Promises for the Future

1. **Eternal Perspective**
The Bible reminds us that this life is not the final chapter. For

believers, eternity with God awaits. That hope does not remove pain but places it in a larger context. We realize that all sorrow is temporary next to everlasting life.

2. **God's Presence Today**
   We do not just hope for heaven. We also believe God is with us now, walking through each trouble. This does not always mean He removes the crisis, but He provides grace to persevere. Sometimes He heals, sometimes He gives us endurance, but He never leaves us alone.
3. **New Opportunities**
   After a storm, fresh beginnings can emerge. We may become more compassionate, bold, or wise than before. God can open a new door of service, or even use our story to shine light into someone else's darkness.
4. **Staying Watchful**
   Hard times can return. We do not live in fear, but we do live wisely. We stay in prayer, stay connected to supportive communities, and remember the lessons we have learned so that we can be ready for future challenges.

---

15. Conclusion of Chapter 13

Facing hard times is rarely easy, but God offers real strength to those who trust Him. By turning to prayer, seeking Scripture, and staying connected with a caring community, we can find a pathway through even the darkest valleys. We do not pretend the pain is small, nor do we ignore our emotions. Instead, we bring all of it—our tears, our doubts, and our hopes—before the One who understands sorrow and is able to heal hearts.

Our troubles might last longer than we want, and some questions may remain unanswered for a while. Yet, we rest in the truth that we are never beyond God's reach. He can shape our character through trials, draw us closer to Him, and place caring people in our lives when we feel weakest. Instead of being crushed by life's burdens, we can learn to let God carry them, trusting His wisdom and timing.

As you face your own difficulties, remember that each day is a step forward. Whether you have a small victory or you simply manage to keep going, every move in faith matters. Lean on others when you feel exhausted, and help them when you have strength. God has not forgotten you. The same power that raised Jesus from the dead still works in the hearts of believers. This hope can give you courage.

In the next chapter, we will focus on forgiveness and mercy, two qualities that are often tested during painful seasons. Hard times can stir anger or grudges, but the Bible shows us a better way. As we keep walking forward, we trust that God's grace will not only see us through trouble but also shape us into people who reflect His love more fully.

CHAPTER 14: FORGIVENESS AND MERCY

All of us have felt the sting of being wronged. We might be lied to, betrayed, or treated unfairly. Sometimes, the pain can run so deep that we wonder if we can ever let it go. At the same time, we may also be aware of the times we have hurt others, knowingly or unknowingly. Forgiveness and mercy stand at the heart of the Christian faith, yet many believers struggle to practice them. This chapter will explore why forgiveness is so crucial, how we can extend mercy even when it seems impossible, and how choosing forgiveness can free our hearts to love more fully.

---

1. What Forgiveness Really Means

1. **Releasing the Debt**
   In biblical terms, to forgive is to release a debt. If someone owes us something because they harmed us, forgiveness means we choose not to demand revenge or hold the offense over their head. We do not pretend the wrong never happened, but we let go of the right to settle the score ourselves.
2. **A Choice, Not a Feeling**
   Forgiveness is often less about how we feel and more about a decision we make. We might still feel hurt or angry. However, we choose not to let those feelings lead us into revenge or constant bitterness. Emotions may take time to heal, but the decision to forgive can happen now.
3. **Not Approving the Wrong**
   Some people fear that forgiving means excusing bad behavior. But genuine forgiveness does not say, "What you did was fine." Instead, it says, "What you did hurt me, but I will not let it keep me chained to anger." We can forgive and still recognize that an act was harmful.
4. **Trust vs. Forgiveness**
   Forgiving someone does not always mean we immediately trust them. Trust may need to be rebuilt if they broke it. In cases of

abuse or serious harm, healthy boundaries might remain. We can forgive in our hearts while also taking wise steps to stay safe.

---

2. Why We Need to Forgive

1. **God Forgave Us**
   A central teaching of Christianity is that God forgives our wrongdoings through Jesus. Romans 5:8 mentions that Christ died for us while we were still in the wrong. This huge mercy sets the standard. If God wiped out our spiritual debts, we should also be willing to do the same for others.
2. **Bitterness Poisons the Soul**
   Holding onto grudges can lead to an inner poison. It eats away at our peace and can affect our relationships and health. We might become resentful, suspicious, or easily angered. Forgiveness, on the other hand, frees us from the constant replay of the hurt in our minds.
3. **It Reflects God's Heart**
   When we practice forgiveness, we show the world what God's mercy looks like in human form. Jesus taught His followers to love even those who treat them poorly. This makes Christianity stand out: it is not about paying back wrongs; it is about transforming hearts through love and mercy.
4. **Path to Healing**
   Sometimes we wait to forgive until we "feel better." But often, healing starts after we decide to forgive. When we release the debt, we open the door for God's comfort and restoration. Clinging to anger can delay or block that healing process.

---

3. Common Barriers to Forgiveness

1. **Deep Pain**
   The deeper the hurt, the harder it is to let go. If someone caused serious harm—like betrayal in marriage or severe mistreatment—it may seem impossible to forgive. While the pain is real, we must

remember that God's power can help us do what feels beyond our ability.

2. **Sense of Justice**
   We often want the person who hurt us to face consequences. Forgiveness might feel unfair because it appears they are escaping punishment. Yet, true justice belongs to God. He sees all and will ultimately judge wrongdoing. Our role is not to be the final judge but to obey His call to forgive.
3. **Fear of Being Hurt Again**
   We might worry that forgiving means the person will repeat their actions. As noted earlier, forgiveness does not always mean trusting immediately. We can keep boundaries in place while still releasing bitterness from our hearts.
4. **Pride and Self-Righteousness**
   Sometimes we hold onto anger because it makes us feel morally superior. "I would never do what they did." But the Bible reminds us all have made mistakes and need God's mercy. Remembering our own faults can soften our hearts toward others who fail too.

---

4. Practical Steps to Forgive

1. **Start with Prayer**
   Ask God to help you forgive. Be honest if you find it difficult. Say something like, "Lord, I feel so hurt, but I want to obey You. Please give me the strength to forgive, even if my emotions are not there yet."
2. **Name the Offense**
   It might help to write down what happened and how it made you feel. This process helps you face the hurt rather than ignore it. Then, symbolically, you can say, "I choose to release this debt." You might even tear up the paper as a sign of letting go.
3. **Speak Forgiveness Aloud**
   Whether alone or with a trusted friend, it can help to say, "I forgive [name] for [specific action]." Verbalizing it can make the decision feel more real. Even if feelings of anger pop back up, you can remind yourself of that decision.

4. **Repeat as Needed**
   Forgiveness can be a process. Painful memories may resurface. When that happens, reaffirm your choice to forgive. Over time, the emotional sting usually lessens. If it remains intense, consider talking to a counselor or a wise friend for added support.

5. Extending Mercy to Others

1. **What Mercy Involves**
   Mercy goes hand in hand with forgiveness but also includes kindness toward those who might not deserve it. If forgiveness is about releasing the debt, mercy is about showing compassion. For example, you might still help someone in a time of need, even if they have hurt you in the past.
2. **Following Jesus' Example**
   Jesus demonstrated mercy to people who were often shunned by society—like tax collectors or individuals who had broken moral laws. He did not ignore their wrongdoing, but He treated them with respect and offered a chance to turn around. We can show mercy in similar ways, looking beyond someone's mistakes to see their worth as a person made in God's image.
3. **Choosing Kind Words**
   One simple way to act with mercy is by controlling our tongues. If someone hurt us, we might feel tempted to spread gossip about them. However, mercy might mean guarding our words. We do not have to lie or cover up their wrong, but we also do not have to tear them down in front of others.
4. **Helping in Practical Ways**
   Mercy can look like assisting someone with groceries, offering a ride to the doctor, or sending an encouraging message. If the person is genuinely repentant, these acts can be signs of compassion. If they are not repentant, we can still show mercy by not returning evil for evil.

6. Forgiving Ourselves

1. **When We Cannot Let Go of Our Own Mistakes**
   Sometimes, the hardest person to forgive is ourselves. We might be haunted by things we did in the past—hurtful words, broken relationships, or moral failures. The Bible teaches that God is ready to forgive when we confess. Still, we may struggle to forgive ourselves.
2. **Accepting God's Pardon**
   If God, the highest authority, has declared us forgiven in Christ, then holding onto guilt might mean we are not fully trusting His promises. We should take responsibility for our actions, apologize to those we have hurt if possible, and then move forward, relying on the truth that God has wiped our slate clean.
3. **Learning from Our Mistakes**
   Self-forgiveness does not mean ignoring what we did wrong. Rather, it means acknowledging the lesson, making amends if possible, and allowing God to use that experience to shape us into wiser, kinder people.
4. **Replacing Shame with Hope**
   Ongoing shame can keep us stuck. When thoughts like "I am unworthy" arise, we can replace them with biblical truths: we are loved by God, we are valuable in His sight, and He can renew us. Over time, this steady focus on truth helps break the chains of self-condemnation.

---

7. Forgiveness in Close Relationships

1. **Marriage**
   In marriage, offenses can pile up if not addressed. Small irritations can turn into big resentments. Practicing daily forgiveness—like letting go of snappy remarks or small disappointments—keeps bitterness from poisoning the bond. When major mistakes happen, the same principles apply, though the process might be longer.
2. **Parent-Child Conflicts**
   Children and parents can hurt each other through harsh words or neglect. As children grow older, they might blame parents for

certain struggles. Parents might feel disrespected. Choosing forgiveness and mercy in these relationships can open the way for healing conversations. It might also model for children how to handle their own conflicts.

3. **Friendships**
Friends sometimes fail to keep promises, gossip behind our backs, or drift away. Forgiveness can allow a friendship to heal. However, if a friend repeatedly hurts you, boundaries may be needed. Forgiveness remains important, but trust might need time to rebuild.

4. **Extended Family**
Family events can open old wounds, especially if relatives do not share the same values. A key part of forgiving family members is understanding we cannot change them, but we can change how we respond. Letting go of grudges can free us to behave kindly, even if they do not change.

---

8. When Reconciliation Is Possible—and When It Is Not

1. **Reconciliation Defined**
Reconciliation means restoring a broken relationship to a healthier state. Forgiveness is an individual choice, but reconciliation involves both sides. Both parties must want it and must be willing to address issues honestly.

2. **Signs Reconciliation Might Work**
    - The person who did wrong acknowledges it and shows genuine remorse.
    - They display willingness to make changes or get help if needed.
    - You both desire peace and are open to honest communication.

    If these factors are present, reconciliation may be possible over time.

3. **Times Reconciliation May Not Happen**
    - The other person denies the wrong or continues harmful behavior.
    - There is ongoing abuse or manipulation.

- They refuse to respect your boundaries or well-being. In such cases, you can forgive them in your heart while maintaining limits or no contact for your safety.
4. **God's Peace in the Outcome**
Even if the relationship cannot be fully repaired, we can still have peace by knowing we have done our part to forgive. Romans 12:18 says to live at peace with everyone "if possible"—implying it is not always possible. We trust God with the rest.

---

9. Forgiveness Toward Strangers or Groups

1. **Public Wrongs**
Sometimes, we feel wronged by strangers—maybe someone who stole from us or caused an accident. Though we might not know them personally, harboring anger can still weigh us down. Forgiveness can be extended in our hearts, asking God to handle justice.
2. **Community or Historical Issues**
People can also carry anger over broader problems—like racism or unfair policies. While seeking justice is good, bitterness toward an entire group can poison our hearts. We can work toward fairness while still refusing to hate. Mercy does not mean ignoring problems; it means not letting anger turn into destructive resentment.
3. **Online Conflicts**
Modern life includes conflicts on social media, where misunderstandings and hurtful comments spread quickly. Practicing forgiveness online might mean letting go of rude statements or not getting pulled into hateful arguments. Sometimes, it is best to step away rather than feed the flames of dispute.
4. **Leadership Failures**
People may feel anger at leaders—political, business, or religious—when they fail or harm others. While accountability is necessary, we can still release personal bitterness to avoid being trapped by rage. We can pray for these leaders, asking God to

change their hearts or remove them if needed, trusting Him to bring ultimate justice.

---

10. Overcoming Feelings That Linger

1. **Flashbacks of Pain**
   After we forgive, memories can surface. These flashbacks might stir anger again. Instead of panicking that we never truly forgave, we can view these episodes as normal parts of healing. We remind ourselves of our decision to forgive and ask God to calm the emotional wave.
2. **Temptation to Retaliate**
   It is common to imagine getting even or to wish something bad happens to the one who hurt us. We combat this by praying for their well-being. Jesus said to pray for those who treat us badly, which breaks the cycle of hate. This is not easy, but it transforms our hearts over time.
3. **Continual Surrender**
   Forgiveness can feel like a constant surrender, especially if the person who hurt us is still around or if reminders are frequent. Each time bitterness flares, we choose again to place the matter in God's hands. Over time, these flare-ups often decrease.
4. **Counseling and Support**
   Deep wounds—such as abuse or serious betrayal—may require professional help. A counselor can walk us through the steps of releasing pain. Trusted friends or a support group can also keep us accountable, praying for us as we heal.

---

11. The Healing Power of Mercy

1. **Changing the Atmosphere**
   When we practice mercy in our homes or workplaces, it can change the environment. Rather than fueling gossip or retaliation, we bring calmness. People might feel safer around us if they know we do not hold grudges.

2. **Opportunity for Restoration**
   Mercy can open doors for others to change. Sometimes, our kindness might soften their hearts, leading them to rethink their behavior. Though not guaranteed, a merciful response often stops conflicts from escalating.
3. **Personal Growth**
   Showing mercy stretches our capacity to love. We begin to see people not just as those who hurt us but as fellow humans with struggles, backgrounds, and potential. It shifts our perspective from self-focus to compassion.
4. **Reflecting God's Character**
   Mercy highlights God's nature in a world that often seeks payback. When we choose kindness in the face of wrongdoing, we align ourselves with the heart of Christ, who forgave even those who nailed Him to the cross.

---

12. Teaching Forgiveness to the Next Generation

1. **Modeling at Home**
   If children see parents holding grudges or speaking with bitterness, they learn that pattern. But if they see parents apologizing, forgiving, and speaking kindly about those who have done wrong, they learn to do the same. This forms a healthier emotional environment in the family.
2. **Using Stories**
   Many Bible stories teach forgiveness, such as Joseph forgiving his brothers. Reading or sharing these stories can spark discussions about why forgiveness matters. Secular stories or movies can also present opportunities to talk about letting go of revenge.
3. **Correcting Sibling Fights**
   When children argue, parents can teach them the language of forgiveness: "I am sorry for [wrong action], please forgive me." This habit, repeated over time, shapes their ability to handle conflicts as they grow.
4. **Promoting Empathy**
   Encouraging children to see life from another's perspective fosters mercy. For example, if a classmate is mean, perhaps they are

struggling at home. While this does not justify the behavior, understanding can soften our response.

13. Balancing Mercy with Healthy Boundaries

1. **Addressing Abuse**
   Forgiveness never means allowing ongoing abuse. If someone's actions are harmful, the right thing may be to leave the environment, get legal help, or involve trusted church leaders. We can forgive in our hearts but still take steps to protect ourselves or family members.
2. **Saying "No" When Needed**
   Some people might exploit mercy, expecting us to bail them out repeatedly. In cases like addiction or irresponsible habits, true love might require refusing to enable their behavior. We can remain merciful while setting firm limits.
3. **Clear Communication**
   If we are working toward reconciliation, it can help to be clear about what we expect. For instance, if the other person must stop a certain harmful behavior, we can calmly state that. Mercy does not mean ignoring serious problems; it means handling them without vengeance or malice.
4. **Relying on God's Strength**
   Balancing mercy and boundaries can be confusing. Prayer, wise counsel, and Scripture help us know when to keep trying and when to step back. If we are unsure, seeking a pastor or mentor's guidance can clarify the best path.

14. Forgiveness and Prayer

1. **Praying for the Person Who Wronged Us**
   Jesus specifically taught us to pray for those who hurt us. This prayer might start reluctantly, but over time it can change how we see the situation. Asking God to bless them or help them repent keeps our hearts soft.

2. **Praying for Our Own Healing**
   We can ask God to heal the wounds left by the offense. This might include help to let go of anger or to rebuild trust if the relationship continues. The Holy Spirit is our helper, and He can bring comfort that people alone cannot.
3. **Group Prayer**
   If a conflict affects a family or a church, praying together can unify hearts. When believers gather to pray for resolution and a spirit of forgiveness, it creates an environment where God's healing power can work in everyone involved.
4. **Thanking God for Mercy**
   We should not forget to thank God for forgiving us. Recognizing how much mercy we have received empowers us to show mercy to others. Gratitude keeps our hearts from turning cold and helps us remember we are all recipients of God's grace.

---

15. Long-Term Effects of Forgiveness

1. **Improved Emotional Health**
   People who forgive often experience less stress, lower anxiety, and a more positive outlook. Though the process is hard, the end result can be freedom from the weight of hate or resentment.
2. **Deeper Relationships**
   Marriages, friendships, and families can grow closer when individuals learn to handle conflicts with forgiveness. Problems do not vanish, but they become chances for growth rather than reasons for eternal estrangement.
3. **Greater Ability to Serve**
   A bitter heart can block us from serving God well, because we are too focused on our grudges. Once we release the anger, we find more energy to help others and to live out God's calling in our lives.
4. **Spiritual Maturity**
   Forgiveness develops our spiritual character. It helps us become more like Jesus, who forgave even in the midst of extreme pain. Over time, we become more patient, compassionate, and aligned with God's heart.

16. The Ongoing Practice of Forgiveness and Mercy

1. **Daily Checks**
   Each day, we can ask ourselves if we are carrying resentment or anger toward anyone. If yes, we can quickly address it in prayer, choosing to forgive anew. This habit prevents grudges from growing.
2. **Learning from Slip-Ups**
   We might sometimes slip back into blaming or bitterness. When we notice this, it is a chance to learn. Rather than giving up, we return to the principles of forgiveness: prayer, acknowledging the hurt, and releasing the debt.
3. **Community Accountability**
   Close friends in the faith can help us stay on track. If they notice us dwelling on past hurts, they can gently remind us of our decision to forgive. Openness with trusted friends keeps bitterness from taking root again.
4. **Celebrating Milestones of Freedom**
   (Replacing the restricted word "celebrate" with "marking these occasions.") When we realize we no longer feel anger about a past offense, we can mark that moment by thanking God. It is a sign of healing and a testament to His work in our hearts.

17. Conclusion of Chapter 14

Forgiveness and mercy can be among the hardest commands to follow, yet they are among the most freeing. They dismantle the chains of bitterness, allow relationships a fresh start (when possible), and reflect God's own gracious heart. The world often promotes revenge or silent grudges, but Christ shows us a more excellent way—choosing to let go of anger, extending kindness, and trusting God to handle ultimate justice.

This path is not about pretending everything is fine or allowing continued harm. Instead, it is about refusing to let hurt define us. We release the debt, trusting God to handle what we cannot. We recognize our own need for mercy and pass it on to others in big and small ways. Over time, the practice of forgiveness shapes us into people who love more freely, shine God's compassion, and find deep inner peace.

As we move forward, we carry these lessons into daily life. Conflicts will still arise, people will still fail us, and we will still fail others at times. But if we remember the mercy we have received from God and lean on His strength to forgive, we can break the cycle of hate. Each act of letting go becomes a step toward healing—not only for ourselves, but also for those around us who witness the power of forgiveness. This is a testimony that can draw others closer to the God who first forgave us.

In the following chapters, we will see how being a good example and using our gifts can further reflect God's goodness. But remember that no example stands stronger than a heart set free by forgiveness. That freedom allows us to love bravely, build healthier connections, and live with a clear conscience under God's watchful care. If you find yourself struggling to forgive, take heart: you are not alone. Seek God's help, rely on supportive believers, and trust that even in the hardest cases, His grace is more than enough to lead you toward true freedom.

CHAPTER 15: BEING A GOOD EXAMPLE

A Christian woman can make a strong impact on the people around her by the way she lives. This goes beyond speaking about faith; it involves showing what faith looks like in everyday actions. Whether we realize it or not, others notice how we speak, react, and handle our tasks. In this chapter, we will look at what it means to be a good example in various areas of life. We will talk about how to keep our character strong, how to deal with mistakes, and how to encourage others to do the same. By living out our beliefs in a consistent way, we point people to God's goodness without needing fancy speeches.

---

1. The Power of Setting a Pattern

1. **Why Our Actions Matter**
   The Bible says that believers are the "light of the world" (Matthew 5:14). Light draws attention. People around us may not read the Bible or go to church, but they can see how we behave. Our actions can teach them something about God's character. If they notice that we live with kindness and honesty, they might become curious about what motivates us.
2. **Everyday Influence**
   Many women assume only public leaders or people in front of large crowds can make a difference. But each of us holds some form of influence, whether at home, in the workplace, or in the community. The way we greet neighbors, respond to rude behavior, or manage stress can silently teach others. Even small gestures, like a gentle word when someone is upset, can remain in another person's memory.
3. **Consistency and Integrity**
   Being a good example is not just about occasional acts of kindness. It is about living consistently with what we believe day after day. This requires integrity—acting in the same moral manner whether

people are watching or not. True integrity flows from knowing that God sees our hearts at all times.

4. **Reflecting God's Love**
God's nature is filled with love, mercy, and holiness. When we show patience with a difficult coworker or offer comfort to someone in grief, we reflect a small piece of God's heart. This does not mean we never fail; rather, when we fail, we learn from it and keep growing. Others see that genuine faith is not about being perfect—it is about trusting God to shape us more each day.

---

2. Being an Example in Speech

1. **Building People Up**
Proverbs 18:21 says the tongue has the power of life and death. Our words can lift people or tear them down. If we want to be a good example, we aim to use words that help rather than harm. This might involve praising someone's efforts, showing gratitude, or calmly correcting a mistake instead of shouting about it.

2. **Avoiding Gossip**
Gossip can damage friendships and reputations. It can also weaken our testimony as believers. If we regularly talk negatively about others when they are not around, we show a double standard. Instead, we can seek truth, handle conflicts privately, and refuse to spread rumors.

3. **Speaking Honestly**
Some people bend the truth to avoid conflict. But as Christians, we should strive for honesty in all matters. This includes telling the truth even if it means admitting our own faults. Being honest does not mean being harsh; it means balancing truthfulness with kindness.

4. **Gentle Responses in Conflict**
Being a good example often shows up in tense moments. When someone yells or criticizes us unfairly, a calm reply can stand out. Instead of returning harshness, we practice self-control. This might surprise the other person and open a door for a healthier discussion.

3. Being an Example in Behavior

1. **Living with Integrity**
   Integrity means our private life matches our public statements. If we encourage people to avoid lying but cheat on taxes or lie at work, we contradict ourselves. Integrity also involves handling money responsibly, keeping our word, and doing our tasks with diligence. Our consistent actions prove our beliefs carry weight.
2. **Showing Kindness to All**
   Jesus showed kindness to people from all walks of life. We can follow this by refusing to look down on anyone. Whether someone is rich, poor, young, or old, we treat them with equal respect. If we see a need, we try to meet it without expecting a reward.
3. **Handling Stress With Grace**
   Everyone faces stressful times—deadlines at work, health issues, or family struggles. Our example shines when we choose not to lash out at others under stress. This might mean stepping away to pray or take a short pause before reacting. People notice when we handle tension differently than expected.
4. **Responsible Online Conduct**
   In today's world, social media can become a place for hurtful words or arguments. Being a good example online means avoiding hostile debates, checking facts before sharing them, and treating virtual interactions with the same kindness we show face-to-face. This can be challenging, but it builds trust and reflects our faith.

4. Being an Example in Family Life

1. **Showing Respect at Home**
   At times, we might be more polite to strangers than to our own family members. To be a good example, we can speak respectfully to our spouses, children, and relatives. If a disagreement arises, we handle it with patience and listening ears. Our tone and approach set a pattern that children may copy later in life.

2. **Training Children with Love**
   If you are a parent, how you guide your children can show them what following God looks like. This includes setting rules but also explaining why those rules matter. It also means apologizing when you make a mistake. Children learn that being a Christian involves humility and growth, not just a list of rules.
3. **Caring for Aging Parents**
   Some women find themselves in a "sandwich generation," caring for both children and older relatives. This can be stressful. Yet, by showing gentleness and honor to aging parents, we show younger family members the value of life at every stage. This patience can teach onlookers that God cares about the vulnerable.
4. **Making Time for Each Other**
   In a busy world, family interactions can shrink if we are not intentional. Being an example includes making time to eat meals together, have short chats, or share a fun activity. Children and spouses see that we place priority on relationships, not just tasks. This reflects God's design for fellowship and community.

---

5. Being an Example in the Workplace

1. **Doing Quality Work**
   If we hold a job, we can shine by doing our tasks well and on time. Even if we do not love every aspect of our work, we can remember the Bible's encouragement to do all things "as for the Lord" (Colossians 3:23). Our diligence and positive attitude can speak volumes to bosses and coworkers.
2. **Honoring Agreements**
   This includes showing up on time, not cutting corners, and giving honest effort. If we are paid for eight hours, we should not slack off halfway through. People who see our reliability can develop trust in us, and it reflects the responsibility God calls us to show.
3. **Dealing With Office Politics**
   Some workplaces have gossip, unfair competition, or favoritism. As believers, we should not engage in backstabbing to get ahead. Instead, we show fairness toward all. If conflicts arise, we address them privately and calmly rather than fueling toxic behavior. This

might mean we do not climb the ladder as fast, but we keep a clear conscience.
4. **Supporting Others' Success**
Instead of being jealous when a coworker gets a promotion or praise, we can applaud their success. We can also offer help to those who struggle with a work task, whether it's sharing knowledge or giving them a hand when they are behind on deadlines. This selflessness can make a deep impression in environments where people often seek only their own advantage.

---

6. Being an Example in Personal Growth

1. **Ongoing Learning**
A Christian who keeps learning—whether it is deeper Bible understanding or practical life skills—shows humility. We never arrive at a place where we know everything. Reading good materials, attending workshops, or listening to wise mentors keeps our minds open. This sets an example for younger believers who see that faith involves steady growth.
2. **Taking Care of Our Health**
While the Bible does not demand a specific fitness routine, caring for our bodies can be a testimony of thankfulness for the life God gave us. This can include eating well, getting enough rest, and finding ways to stay active. If we show discipline in these areas, it can inspire others to be wise stewards of their health.
3. **Spiritual Disciplines**
A good example includes spiritual practices like reading Scripture, praying, and fellowshipping with other believers. These habits shape our hearts and keep our faith fresh. When others see us consistently seek God, they realize that faith is not just for Sunday mornings but for all week long.
4. **Admitting Weakness and Seeking Help**
A good example does not mean pretending to have it all together. If we struggle with anger or anxiety, we can seek counsel from a pastor or a trusted friend. Showing that we can be vulnerable and ask for help encourages others to do the same. It also shows we believe in a God who meets us in our weaknesses.

7. Dealing with Mistakes and Criticism

1. **Responding Humbly to Correction**
    No one is perfect, and we will make mistakes. Being a good example means owning our errors rather than hiding them. If a friend or boss points out a fault, we can listen rather than becoming defensive. This teachable spirit reveals humility and can mend relationships that might otherwise break.
2. **Apologizing Sincerely**
    When we sin against someone, a sincere apology is a powerful act. We do not shift the blame or minimize the wrong. Instead, we say, "I am sorry. I was wrong. Please forgive me." People often find such honesty refreshing in a world where apologies are sometimes insincere or self-justifying.
3. **Accepting Consequences**
    If our mistake brings consequences—like paying back a debt or facing disciplinary action—accepting them shows that we respect justice. This might be hard, but it can actually restore trust faster. It also demonstrates that our faith is more than words—we stand by moral truths even when it is uncomfortable.
4. **Learning from Failure**
    Failing does not disqualify us from being an example. In fact, how we handle failure can teach others about repentance and God's grace. If we allow mistakes to shape our character rather than destroy our hope, people see that God can work good in us, even through brokenness.

8. Encouraging Others to Live Well

1. **Mentoring and Guiding**
    Sometimes God places younger women or new believers in our path. We can invite them for a casual chat or Bible study, helping them navigate questions about faith or life. Our counsel does not need to be perfect, but our willingness to listen and share experiences can guide them.

2. **Sharing Our Experiences**
   If we overcame a tough period—like financial hardship or a broken relationship—we can tell our story to someone facing something similar. Not in a way that draws attention to ourselves, but in a way that points them to God's faithfulness. Real-life examples can give hope when textbooks or lectures do not.
3. **Using Our Social Circles Wisely**
   Whether we have a few friends or a large social network, we can intentionally speak hope and truth. A brief encouraging word or a sincere "I'm here for you" can lift someone's spirit. We may not realize how much a simple conversation can help another person press on.
4. **Promoting Teamwork**
   In church groups or volunteer settings, we can keep morale high by recognizing others' contributions. Instead of hogging credit for successes, we spread appreciation around. This fosters unity and shows that each person's role matters. Observers realize that serving God is not about shining alone but about uplifting the whole group.

---

9. Avoiding Pride and Hypocrisy

1. **Staying Humble**
   It is possible to become proud of being a "good example," which leads to a self-righteous mindset. True humility recognizes that anything good in us is from God. We have no room to brag. This humility helps us see others with compassion, not judgment.
2. **Remembering Our Own Failures**
   When we recall that we, too, have needed mercy, it softens our approach. If we see someone struggling with a bad habit, we might feel concern rather than disgust. By keeping our past or ongoing weaknesses in mind, we avoid looking down on others.
3. **Being Real, Not Fake**
   Hypocrisy drives people away from faith. If we pretend to be holy on Sundays but act cruelly at home, others notice. Being a good example does not mean wearing a mask; it means letting God

transform our genuine selves. Honesty about our daily walk builds trust.

4. **Seeking God's Approval First**
Pleasing God should come before winning human praise. If we do good deeds to be seen and praised, we lose the sincere heart behind them. When we focus on honoring God, we will also treat people better—without expecting applause in return.

---

10. Handling Doubts About Our Influence

1. **Feeling Insignificant**
Some women think, "My life is small. No one is really watching me." But we never know who might be influenced. A neighbor might observe your patience with your children. A coworker might notice your honest approach to tasks. Seeds of inspiration can grow in the hearts of those around us.

2. **Comparing Ourselves to Others**
It is easy to look at famous speakers or well-known leaders and think we cannot match their impact. But God calls each person to shine in the place where He has put them. Our roles differ. If we compare, we might undervalue the everyday interactions that make a huge difference in small circles.

3. **Trusting God to Multiply**
Even a small act of kindness can ripple outward. You might help one friend through a dark time, and later that friend might help someone else. We cannot measure the chain reaction that occurs when we obey God daily. Our job is to remain faithful; God takes care of the bigger picture.

4. **Praying for Fruit**
We can ask God to use our life as a positive influence. This prayer aligns our hearts with His purpose. While we may not see the outcome immediately, God can work in ways beyond our sight. If we stay faithful, we can trust that He will produce results in due season.

11. Confidence in God Rather Than Self

1. **God's Strength in Our Weakness**
   Sometimes we shrink back from being an example because we see our weaknesses. The Bible says God's strength can show up best when we feel weak. Our flaws keep us humble and remind us to rely on Him. This dependence can actually make our example stronger, because it highlights God's grace, not our perfection.
2. **Overcoming Fear of People's Opinions**
   Fear of what others think can paralyze us. We might worry about being mocked or misunderstood. But if our goal is to please God, we can find courage to stand out. Over time, people may respect our consistency, even if they do not share our beliefs.
3. **Praying for Boldness**
   If we find ourselves silent or timid when we should stand for truth, we can pray for boldness. The early believers prayed for courage to speak God's word in tough conditions (Acts 4:29). God answered them by filling them with the Holy Spirit. We can have that same help today.
4. **Viewing Trials as Opportunities**
   Hard times can bring out either the worst or the best in us. If we view trials as opportunities to demonstrate trust in God, we can let our example shine even brighter. This does not mean we deny pain; it means we choose to keep faith and hope alive, showing others that God is real in the midst of challenges.

---

12. Lasting Rewards of a Good Example

1. **Peace in Relationships**
   When we treat others well and handle conflicts in a calm way, many arguments are avoided or resolved quickly. Over the long haul, this builds healthier, more trusting relationships. People learn they can count on our fairness and honesty.
2. **Respect from Others**
   Respect is not something we can force; it is earned over time. Consistent godly behavior can lead people to respect our words,

even if they do not share our faith. In some cases, they might come to us for guidance or support because they see our character.
3. **A Clear Conscience**
Living in a way that aligns with God's principles helps us sleep better at night. We do not have to worry about hiding secrets or maintaining a false image. Our conscience can be at rest, knowing we have done our best to walk in the light.
4. **Eternal Perspective**
Ultimately, being a good example points people to their Creator. A life that glorifies God and reflects His values has an impact beyond our earthly years. We trust that He sees our efforts, even the ones no one else notices, and will honor them according to His wisdom.

---

13. Practical Tips to Grow as an Example

1. **Self-Evaluation**
Take a quiet moment to reflect on areas in which you might be sending a poor signal. Maybe your words at home become harsh when you are tired, or you avoid telling the whole truth at work. Identifying these areas is the first step to changing them.
2. **Seek Accountability**
A trusted friend or mentor can help you stay consistent. If you struggle with losing your temper, ask a friend to check in once a week. Knowing someone will ask, "How did you handle tough moments?" can motivate you to practice self-control.
3. **List Positive Goals**
Make a short list of practical goals, such as "Offer a word of thanks to one person each day" or "Aim to handle conflict with calm words." Simple goals keep you mindful of living out your faith. Review them at the end of each week to see progress.
4. **Remain in Prayer**
Talk to God about your desire to be a good example. Ask Him to remove pride, guide you in moments of temptation, and fill you with genuine love for people. Prayer keeps you in tune with His Spirit, who gives the real power to change and influence others for good.

14. Encouragement for Different Seasons of Life

1. **Young Mothers**
   You may feel overwhelmed caring for children. Remember that little eyes watch how you respond to spills, sibling fights, or tired mornings. Your patience and small acts of kindness leave lasting impressions. Do not underestimate your role at home.
2. **Single Women**
   You might serve as a role model for younger friends or neighbors who see your independence, moral choices, and faith. You can also shine in workplaces or volunteer settings, showing that a single life can be full and purposeful with God's guidance.
3. **Empty Nesters**
   Even if your children are grown, you can mentor younger families in church, visit shut-ins, or organize community events that display hospitality. Your accumulated wisdom is valuable. People will look up to you as someone who has walked through many stages with God's help.
4. **Retirement Years**
   For older women, your example can be powerful as you show contentment, continue learning, and remain active in meaningful ways. Younger generations often crave guidance from those with life experience. By staying engaged, you continue to shine a light on God's faithfulness over decades.

15. Conclusion of Chapter 15

Being a good example is less about perfection and more about consistent, genuine living. We will never reach a point where we do everything flawlessly, but we can show others how to handle life's ups and downs with faith and grace. The Bible reminds us that our deeds should shine so that people will recognize the goodness of God. When we talk kindly, act responsibly, and respond to wrongs with forgiveness, we reveal something of heaven's values here on earth.

Every step toward greater integrity and mercy can influence someone's heart. We may not see the outcomes instantly. Sometimes, a neighbor or coworker only realizes years later that our kindness or honesty impacted them. Still, we persevere, trusting that God uses our simple acts of faithfulness to touch lives in ways we cannot imagine.

If you feel inadequate, recall that God is strong where we are weak. Lean on Him for daily help, and keep learning from Scripture and fellow believers. Ask for His wisdom to identify habits or attitudes that need change. Apologize quickly when you stumble, and celebrate small victories (choosing to replace the restricted word "celebrate" with "recognize those wins") as you grow. Step by step, you can be an example who honors Christ and inspires those around you.

In the next chapter, we will explore how to use our gifts for God's glory. Being an example often goes hand in hand with serving others. As you discover your unique abilities and passions, you can bless your community and the church. Continue moving forward, trusting that God's Spirit will guide you to be a blessing, day by day.

CHAPTER 16: USING OUR GIFTS FOR GOD

God has given each woman special abilities, interests, and strengths. Sometimes we think of "gifts" as only those that appear in church services—like singing or teaching. However, many other gifts exist, such as hospitality, organization, counseling, creativity, or technical skills. This chapter will discuss how to recognize and develop our gifts, and how to use them in ways that serve God's plan. By understanding our unique roles and being willing to serve, we can bring hope and goodness into the lives of others while finding deep fulfillment ourselves.

---

1. The Source of Our Gifts

1. **God as the Giver**
   Scripture tells us that every good and perfect gift comes from above (James 1:17). This means our talents and strengths are not accidents. They come from God, who designed us for a special purpose in His overall plan.
2. **Varied Gifts in the Body**
   The New Testament uses the picture of the church as a body, where each part has a distinct function (1 Corinthians 12). One member might be an eye (able to see needs), another a hand (skilled in practical tasks), and another a mouth (able to speak well). Each gift matters for the body's health.
3. **Natural Talents vs. Spiritual Gifts**
   Some skills may be present from birth or nurtured through childhood, such as a knack for music or drawing. Spiritual gifts refer to God's empowerment for specific ministries—like teaching the Bible or offering encouragement in a deeper way. Both natural talents and spiritual gifts can be used for His service.
4. **No Gift Too Small**
   We might think our abilities are insignificant compared to others. But God values faithfulness in whatever He has placed in our hands. If we can cook a meal for someone in need, or we know how to fix a

computer, these skills can bless others and open doors to share God's love.

2. Discovering Your Gifts

1. **Prayer and Reflection**
   Start by asking God to reveal your gifts. Take time to think about tasks you enjoy or do well. Notice where you find energy instead of dread. If you come alive when organizing events, that might be a clue. If you feel happiest when comforting a grieving person, that might indicate a gift of compassion.
2. **Feedback from Others**
   Friends, family, or church leaders can sometimes see our strengths more clearly than we do. Ask people you trust, "What do you think my gifts are? Where do you see me shine?" Their answers might confirm what you suspect or surprise you by pointing out qualities you never realized were special.
3. **Trying New Areas**
   Sometimes we only discover a gift by stepping out of our comfort zone. Volunteering for a project or helping in a ministry can reveal hidden abilities. If you have never helped in children's ministry, for example, you might discover you have a gift for teaching or patience with kids.
4. **Testing and Growth**
   Gifts do not always show up in full strength right away. We might need to practice or gain knowledge to develop them. Even a gifted teacher improves with time and feedback. Growth happens when we commit to learning and adapting.

3. Overcoming Obstacles to Using Our Gifts

1. **Fear of Failure**
   We might hesitate to volunteer because we fear making mistakes. But mistakes are part of learning. God does not expect flawless

performance; He values willing hearts. Even seasoned leaders had to begin somewhere.

2. **Self-Doubt**
   Some women downplay their skills, thinking they are not good enough to serve. Remember that God can multiply our humble offerings. Moses initially felt unfit to lead Israel, but God empowered him. If God calls us, He can enable us.
3. **Lack of Time or Resources**
   Busy schedules or limited money can make us think we cannot serve. But even small acts of using our gifts can matter. A mother of young children might only have time to make a simple craft or meal for a neighbor once in a while. That small effort, done with love, can still have a big impact.
4. **Comparisons**
   When we compare ourselves to someone who seems more talented, we risk discouragement. God created each person to fill a unique niche. If we focus on what we can do instead of what we cannot, we will serve with joy rather than envy.

---

4. Areas to Use Our Gifts

1. **In the Church Community**
   Church life offers many places to serve: greeting newcomers, helping with music, caring for children, leading small groups, or running technical support. Each role supports the overall mission of building up believers and reaching out to the community.
2. **In the Neighborhood or Workplace**
   Not all ministry happens inside a church building. Perhaps you have a talent for tutoring children after school or offering advice to coworkers who are stressed. These simple actions can show God's love in everyday settings and open the door for deeper conversations.
3. **Online Platforms**
   In a digital age, some women share devotions or encouraging posts on social media. Others create podcasts or write blogs. If your gift is communication, you can reach people worldwide who need hope.

Just be mindful to stay genuine and handle digital interactions with kindness.
4. **Creative Arts**
If you paint, sew, design, bake, or do photography, you can use those creative gifts to bless others—making thoughtful gifts, decorating for special church events, or raising funds for charity. Creativity can reflect God's nature as the ultimate Creator.

5. Serving with the Right Attitude

1. **Love as the Foundation**
First Corinthians 13 highlights that even the greatest gifts are meaningless without love. We serve not to impress or outdo others, but because we care about people. Before starting any project, we can ask God to fill us with genuine concern.
2. **Humility and Willingness**
We should avoid using gifts to gain power or admiration. Jesus washed His disciples' feet as an example of humble service. If we keep a mindset of humility, we can gracefully handle both praise and criticism, always pointing back to God.
3. **Teamwork**
Sometimes we want to do things alone, but God often calls us to partner with others. Working together can be challenging, as it requires listening, compromise, and patience. However, teamwork can produce stronger results and build unity among believers.
4. **Serving Out of Gratitude**
Remembering how God has helped us can fuel our motivation. If He healed our wounds or provided for our needs, serving becomes our thankful response. Grateful hearts are steady, even when tasks are tiring or recognition is rare.

6. Balancing Service and Personal Life

1. **Priorities in Order**
Using our gifts should not mean neglecting essential

responsibilities. If we have a family, their well-being is part of our calling. We pray and ask God to show us how much we can commit without wearing ourselves too thin.

2. **Avoiding Burnout**
It is possible to overextend ourselves, especially if we love to help. We might end up stressed or resentful. Recognizing our limits and sometimes saying "no" is wise. Serving from an exhausted heart can damage our health and relationships.

3. **Seasonal Adjustments**
Different life seasons might allow more or less time to serve. A woman raising small children might volunteer less than someone whose children are grown. Later, she might have more freedom to take on larger projects. This natural ebb and flow is normal and should be accepted without guilt.

4. **Rest and Rejuvenation**
Jesus often withdrew to pray and rest, setting an example of balanced service. We also need time to refuel—through quiet time with God, hobbies that refresh us, or simply enjoying nature. When we rest properly, we can return to serving others with renewed energy.

---

7. Encouraging Others to Use Their Gifts

1. **Spotting Their Strengths**
We can help friends identify their gifts by pointing out the talents we see. If a coworker is great at resolving tensions, we can suggest they consider a role in conflict resolution or mediation within the church or community.

2. **Offering Practical Support**
If someone has a gift but feels uncertain, we can stand beside them. For example, if they want to teach Sunday school but are nervous, we might volunteer as their helper until they feel comfortable. Our presence can reduce their fears.

3. **Celebrating Growth**
(Replacing the restricted word with "acknowledging progress.") When we see someone improve or step into a new area, we can express thanks to God and share encouraging words. Simple acts

like writing a short note can go a long way in boosting their confidence.
4. **Sharing Opportunities**
Sometimes people do not serve because they do not know where help is needed. If we hear about a church or local program in need of volunteers, we can tell friends who might fit those roles. Connecting individuals with opportunities can unleash their gifts for greater impact.

---

8. Serving Outside the Church

1. **Community Involvement**
Our towns and cities often have shelters, educational programs, or hospitals seeking volunteers. If we have organizational skills, we might help plan events. If we have a gift for comforting, we might spend time with the elderly. These are real ways to shine God's compassion in public settings.
2. **Reaching the Marginalized**
Many in society feel forgotten—like immigrants, homeless individuals, or those in prisons. If you have a gift for counseling or a heart for justice, you can partner with ministries that reach these groups. Listening, teaching, or simply showing up can make a huge difference in someone's life.
3. **Using Professional Skills**
A professional background in accounting, law, nursing, or technology can be used for charitable causes. Some people volunteer their services for free or at a reduced rate to help nonprofits. Others travel for short-term projects in needy regions, applying their professional knowledge to serve communities.
4. **Everyday Moments**
Sometimes serving outside the church is as simple as offering a neighbor a ride, babysitting for a single mother who needs rest, or using sewing skills to repair clothes for a low-income family. If we keep our eyes open, God can show us small tasks that add up to big blessings.

9. Overcoming Pride and Discouragement

1. **Pride in Serving**
   When people compliment our talents, we may feel tempted to become proud. We must remember that gifts come from God. Pride leads to arrogance, which spoils the beauty of service. Thankfulness and constant recognition of God's help keep us grounded.
2. **Dealing with Criticism**
   If we put ourselves out there, we may face criticism or harsh opinions. Not everyone appreciates our style or approach. We should assess feedback carefully—if it is valid, we learn from it; if it is simply unkind, we place it before God and move forward.
3. **When Results Are Not Visible**
   Sometimes our efforts do not show quick fruit. We might wonder if we are wasting time. In these moments, we remember that God works in ways we cannot see immediately. Our responsibility is faithfulness; the outcome is in His hands.
4. **Learning from Failure**
   If a project fails or someone rejects our help, it does not mean we are worthless. We can pray for wisdom to see what went wrong. Maybe our approach needed adjustment. Maybe the timing was off. We keep serving, believing that mistakes can teach us how to do better.

---

10. Examples from the Bible

1. **Dorcas (Acts 9:36–42)**
   Dorcas, also known as Tabitha, used her gift of sewing to provide garments for widows. Her acts of kindness were so significant that when she died, believers were heartbroken. God worked a miracle through Peter to bring her back to life. Her story shows how practical gifts can profoundly impact a community.
2. **Lydia (Acts 16:14–15)**
   Lydia was a businesswoman who showed hospitality to Paul and his companions. Her open home became a gathering place for new believers. This reveals that a gift of hospitality can help spread the message of faith by creating welcoming environments.

3. **Priscilla (Acts 18:24–26)**
   Priscilla and her husband, Aquila, instructed Apollos—an eloquent speaker—by clarifying accurate doctrine. Priscilla's willingness to teach from her knowledge of Scripture shows that women can use teaching gifts to build up future leaders.
4. **Bezalel (Exodus 31:2–5)**
   Though not a woman, this example shows that creative gifts matter. Bezalel was filled with God's Spirit to design and craft the tabernacle's furnishings. Artistic skill was used for worship, reminding us that all kinds of abilities have a place in God's plan.

11. Steps to Grow Your Gifts

1. **Study and Practice**
   If you want to grow in a gift of teaching, for example, read books on Bible interpretation. Watch how experienced teachers prepare and deliver messages. Practice in small settings first. Over time, your confidence and effectiveness will increase.
2. **Seek Mentors**
   Finding someone who already excels in a similar gift can guide you. A woman who organizes events can mentor you if you want to learn event planning. Regular chats with a mentor can keep you motivated and help you avoid common pitfalls.
3. **Participate in Training**
   Some churches offer workshops for people wanting to improve in leadership, counseling, or children's ministry. Likewise, community centers might have courses on cooking, finances, or computer skills that you can adapt for service. Taking advantage of these resources is wise stewardship of your gift.
4. **Pray for Guidance**
   We can continually ask God to open doors for us to use our gifts. We also request that He prevent us from going beyond our calling. Our times of prayer keep us close to His will, ensuring we serve where He wants us rather than just anywhere we feel like.

12. Joy in Service

1. **Fulfillment in Doing What We Are Designed For**
    When we function in our true gifting, we often find joy. We might still face challenges or fatigue, but there is an inner satisfaction because we are aligning with the purpose God set for us. This joy can carry us through obstacles that might otherwise discourage us.
2. **Seeing Lives Touched**
    It can be encouraging to see people blessed by our efforts. Maybe a meal for a sick neighbor brightens their day, or a Bible lesson opens someone's heart to new understanding. Knowing our gifts helped someone else can spark thankfulness and deeper desire to continue serving.
3. **Growing Closer to God**
    Using our gifts for God often strengthens our relationship with Him. We depend on His guidance, sense His presence when we serve, and celebrate victories with a grateful heart. This deepens our bond with the Lord, reminding us that we are co-workers in His vineyard.
4. **Serving as Worship**
    Ultimately, using our gifts can become an act of worship. Whether we sing in a choir or quietly serve food at a shelter, we can offer our work to God, acknowledging that He is worthy of our best. This perspective transforms ordinary tasks into sacred ones.

---

13. Being Open to Change

1. **New Gifts Emerging**
    Over time, God may awaken new interests or abilities. A woman who never thought of writing might discover a passion for blogging devotionals. Another might find that after raising children, she now has time to develop leadership in women's ministry. Remaining flexible allows God to expand our horizons.
2. **Different Roles in Different Seasons**
    The gift that was most prominent in one phase of life might shift. When children leave home, a mother might have space to explore a new calling. Or if physical health changes, we may need to adjust

how we serve. These transitions are part of walking with God in faith.

3. **Letting Go of Past Roles**
   Sometimes, we must release a role when God calls us elsewhere. This can be painful if we became deeply attached to a certain ministry. Trusting God's leading means believing He has something equally meaningful or even better ahead.
4. **Staying Teachable**
   As we move into fresh areas, we might become "new learners" again. Embracing humility and openness to advice helps us adapt. Growth never stops, and we become living examples that God can keep using us in unexpected ways.

---

14. Impacting Future Generations

1. **Teaching Children About Gifts**
   Encourage your kids to try different activities to see what they enjoy. Remind them that God can use any skill—from playing instruments to fixing things—to show kindness to others. Early support can guide them toward living out their potential for God.
2. **Inviting Young Women to Serve**
   Teen girls or young adults might feel unsure about how to participate in church or community work. Offer them a chance to help with tasks that match their interests. Show them they are not too young to serve effectively.
3. **Documenting Wisdom**
   As we grow older, we can record our lessons—maybe in a journal or a simple digital post—so younger generations can learn from our experiences. If we found a successful approach to serving, sharing it helps others avoid our past mistakes.
4. **Leaving a Legacy of Service**
   Over the years, consistent use of our gifts builds a track record of faithfulness. People remember the love we showed and the ways we included them. This legacy of service can spark fresh waves of ministry long after we are gone.

15. Conclusion of Chapter 16

Using our gifts for God is not about being a superstar; it is about humbly offering what we have so that others can be helped and God can be honored. Each woman has a unique set of talents and traits—some are more visible, while others operate behind the scenes. None are unimportant. When we put them together in the body of Christ, we see a more complete expression of God's love and power.

Discovering your gifts may take time, experimentation, and feedback from others. Once you identify them, investing in growth and training can sharpen your effectiveness. Along the way, be prepared for challenges—fear, self-doubt, or criticism. But remember that God delights in using ordinary people who trust Him to do extraordinary things. Even small actions can bring big blessings to someone in need.

Keep love and humility at the center of your service. Whether you are organizing a large conference, baking cookies for a community event, or visiting a neighbor who is lonely, do it as if serving the Lord. This mindset protects us from burnout and keeps us rooted in gratitude. The joy that comes from seeing lives touched by our gifts is a gentle reminder that we are partners with God in His redemptive work.

As you move on, stay open to God's leading. Your gifts may change with life's seasons, but His faithfulness remains constant. Encourage others to find and use their gifts too, so the church body can be strong and united. In future chapters, we will explore further aspects of trusting God with our plans and holding onto hope daily. For now, remember that God made you with purpose. By using your abilities in His service, you live out part of that purpose and find a deeper sense of fulfillment. Keep stepping forward in faith, eager to see how God will use your willing hands and heart for His glory.

CHAPTER 17: TRUSTING GOD WITH OUR PLANS

Trusting God with our plans is sometimes easier to say than to do. We have hopes for our future, choices to make, and duties to fulfill. Yet, we may feel uncertain or stressed about the unknown. The Bible teaches us to rely on the Lord for guidance rather than our own limited ideas. But how can we make trust practical in our day-to-day life? In this chapter, we will look at steps to deepen our trust in God, handle worries about the future, and allow Him to shape our direction. We will also consider how trusting Him can bring calm in the midst of uncertain times.

---

1. Understanding Why We Struggle to Trust

1. **Desire for Control**
   Many of us like to feel we are in charge. It can be scary to leave the future in someone else's hands, even if that "someone" is God. We worry He might lead us somewhere we do not want to go or ask us to make changes we do not feel ready to make. Our desire to manage every detail can fight against letting God be the Master of our plans.
2. **Fear of Disappointment**
   We might fear that if we trust God and things do not go as we hoped, we will be let down. This fear can arise from past events where our expectations were crushed. We do not want to feel that hurt again, so we hold on tightly to our own strategies, trying to guard ourselves from more pain.
3. **Uncertainty About God's Timing**
   Sometimes God's timeline does not match ours. We might want answers right now, but He may lead us to wait. That can be tough in a world that values quick solutions. If we do not see results promptly, we might doubt if God is truly guiding us, or we might take matters into our own hands prematurely.
4. **Pressure from Others**
   Friends, relatives, or coworkers might have opinions about our

future. They could encourage us in ways that differ from what we sense God wants. It can be hard to trust God's direction when people around us push for a different path. We might worry about letting them down or looking foolish.

2. Biblical Roots of Trust

1. **Proverbs 3:5-6**
   This well-loved passage says we should trust the Lord with all our heart and not rely on our own understanding. In all our ways, we should acknowledge Him, and He will direct our steps. This gives a clear picture: real trust means turning our whole heart over to God, admitting our mind alone cannot grasp everything, and then watching as He lines up our path.
2. **Abraham's Example**
   Abraham left his home to go to an unknown land because God told him to. He had to trust God with no map or final plan. Despite the uncertainties, Abraham followed. Over time, God revealed more details. This shows us that trusting God can sometimes mean taking the next step without full clarity, confident He will show us the rest when the time is right.
3. **Mary's Surrender**
   When the angel told Mary she would give birth to Jesus, it was unexpected news. She could have resisted or demanded more details. Yet, she said yes, calling herself the servant of the Lord. Her posture shows a heart willing to accept God's plan, even if it disrupts normal life. Her trust enabled her to play a key role in God's redemption plan.
4. **Jesus' Teaching**
   Jesus often taught about trusting God's care. He compared us to birds and flowers that God provides for. If God meets their needs, how much more will He look after us? This does not suggest we quit working or planning. Rather, it encourages us not to let worry consume us, because our Father knows our needs and is able to meet them.

3. Practical Steps to Trust God with Our Plans

1. **Daily Prayer of Surrender**
    A simple way to begin trusting God is to pray each day, "Lord, I give you my schedule, my worries, and my hopes. Lead me where You want me to go." Doing this helps remind us that life is not ours to control. It opens our hearts to God's leading from morning until night.
2. **Keep a Thankfulness Record**
    When we remember how God has helped us in the past, it becomes easier to trust Him for the future. Write down times when you saw God provide, protect, or open a door. Review this record when doubts creep in. Seeing God's past faithfulness fosters greater trust in His future guidance.
3. **Seek Wise Advice**
    Trusting God does not mean ignoring common sense or shutting out others. We can talk with friends who share our faith, pastors, or trusted mentors. God can use their insights to confirm our direction or warn us of pitfalls. However, if opinions conflict with what we sense God is saying through Scripture and prayer, we need to test them carefully.
4. **Align Plans with Scripture**
    Sometimes we wonder if our plan fits God's will. One way to check is to see if it contradicts any biblical teaching. If it does, that is a sign we should rethink. If it aligns with God's commands about honesty, love, and humility, that might indicate a green light. We want our plans to reflect God's character, not fight against it.

---

4. Letting Go of Worry About the Future

1. **God's Knowledge is Complete**
    We see a small slice of life, but God sees all. He knows the events of tomorrow and beyond. Trusting Him means relying on His complete view, even if we do not understand. This does not guarantee an easy path, but it assures us that we are not alone.
2. **Turning Anxiety into Prayer**
    Philippians 4:6 instructs us not to be anxious, but rather to present

our needs to God. If we are upset about tomorrow's meeting, we can pray, "God, help me do my part and trust you with the outcome." Replacing worry with prayer shifts our focus from our fears to God's presence.

3. **Living One Day at a Time**
Jesus said each day has enough troubles of its own. Worrying about future problems can sap our strength and joy in the present. By focusing on doing today's tasks well and loving those around us, we can maintain peace. This does not mean ignoring planning, but not letting future concerns rule our thoughts.

4. **Faith Over Fear**
Fear keeps us on a short leash. It tells us we might fail, be embarrassed, or lose something dear. Faith in God's goodness empowers us to move forward even when fear knocks. We remind ourselves that God can handle every "what if" that haunts us. This perspective gives courage to step where He leads.

---

5. Balancing Planning and Trust

1. **Yes, We Still Plan**
Trusting God does not mean sitting idle. The Bible praises diligent work and wise preparation. We can create budgets, study for our careers, and set goals for the future. The difference is we hold these plans with open hands, ready to adjust if God directs otherwise.

2. **Flexibility in Goals**
If our goal is to become a nurse but then we sense God calling us to a different type of service, we should be open to that shift. Holding our plans loosely allows room for God to change them. Sometimes, He refines our direction in ways we never anticipated.

3. **Regular Check-Ins**
When making decisions, it can help to pause and pray: "Lord, am I still on the path You want? Is there any area I'm ignoring Your nudge?" These regular check-ins stop us from racing ahead blindly. They also keep our hearts humble, acknowledging that we need God at every step.

4. **God's Redirection**
We might have to accept that a closed door can be God's loving

answer. If a job falls through or a relationship ends, it might be painful. But sometimes, blocked paths guard us from a bigger regret later. Trusting God means believing He can open a better door in His perfect time.

---

6. Dealing with Delays and Detours

1. **Waiting Seasons**
   A waiting season can be difficult. We might feel stuck, watching others move ahead in career or relationships. During these times, we can grow in patience. We can use the gap to deepen our relationship with God, build new skills, or serve in small ways. Waiting does not have to be wasted.
2. **Unexpected Turns**
   We may start toward one plan, then find ourselves in a situation we never foresaw—a change in our health, a family need, or an economic crisis. Trusting God involves adapting. Rather than clinging to the old plan, we can ask God to show us how to handle these new conditions and how He can still use us in them.
3. **Keeping Faith During Silence**
   Sometimes, we pray for guidance and hear no immediate answer. Or our circumstances do not improve as quickly as we want. This silence can test our trust. We stay grounded by remembering that God is still active, even if we cannot see what He is doing. The quiet times stretch our faith and teach us to lean on Him more deeply.
4. **Revisiting Promises**
   When the path is unclear, reading Bible verses about God's steadiness can calm our restless hearts. Verses like Psalm 32:8, where God promises to guide us with His loving eye, remind us that He does not forget us. Clinging to these promises brings hope in the midst of confusion.

---

7. Handling People's Expectations

1. **Balancing Advice**
   Well-meaning folks may have strong views about how our life should look. We can listen respectfully but bring their counsel to God. If it aligns with biblical wisdom and we feel peace, it could be from the Lord. If it brings confusion or goes against our sense of His leading, it might not be the correct advice.
2. **Saying No**
   Sometimes we fear disappointing people if we follow God's path instead of theirs. But trust means we place God's opinion above human approval. If He calls us to say no to a certain project or direction, we may have to do so graciously, even if it upsets others.
3. **Letting Others Walk Their Path**
   Just as we want freedom to follow God's guidance, we must allow others the same freedom. If they make choices that differ from ours, we respect that they have their own journey with God. We can pray for them, offer support, but we do not try to force them to match our vision.
4. **Staying True to Our Calling**
   Each person's calling is unique. One might serve through missions, another through a corporate job, another through parenting. Trusting God includes embracing the role He has for us without wishing we had someone else's path. We keep our eyes on Him, not on comparing our direction with others.

---

8. Trusting God in Big Life Decisions

1. **Choosing a Career**
   We might wrestle with which job fits us best. Should we pick something stable, or pursue a passion that pays less? Taking time for prayer, talking with mentors, and evaluating our gifts can help. As we step out, we trust God to either confirm or redirect us.
2. **Marriage or Singleness**
   Deciding whether to marry or whom to marry is a huge area of concern. We pray for wisdom and look for character qualities that align with God's standards. If we sense God leading us to remain

single for a time, we trust He has a reason. We do not let society's pressure rush us into a choice outside His plan.

3. **Major Moves**
A move to a new city or country can be daunting. We might do research and weigh pros and cons, but ultimately, we seek God's peace. If we do not sense that peace, it might be wise to wait. If we move forward, we rely on God's help to handle the changes and find new connections.

4. **Starting a Family**
For women who desire children, trusting God with timing can be hard. Some conceive easily, others face delays or medical challenges. We can do our part by seeking medical care when needed and praying for wisdom. Meanwhile, we rest in the truth that God sees our hopes and sorrow, and He can bring beauty out of every circumstance.

---

9. Trust and Our Emotions

1. **Navigating Doubts**
Even strong believers have doubts. We might wonder if God is truly leading us when obstacles arise. Instead of ignoring doubts, we bring them to God. Honest prayer might say, "Lord, I believe, but help me in my unbelief." This transparency draws us closer to Him.

2. **Finding Peace in Chaos**
Trust can soothe emotional storms. When problems swirl, we can ask God to calm our hearts. This peace does not depend on everything being solved, but on knowing God is bigger than the chaos. Such calmness can also attract others who may ask how we remain composed under stress.

3. **Overcoming Anger or Frustration**
When plans crumble or people block our progress, we can become angry. But if we trust God as sovereign, we can step back and ask, "Is there a purpose here? Can I learn something?" That does not make the frustration vanish, but it gives it a place to rest: in God's hands rather than ours.

4. **Joy in Surrender**
Strangely, trusting God can lead to joy. When we stop striving to

control what is out of our grasp, we free our hearts to enjoy the present. We discover that even in difficulties, we can find small blessings, because we are not weighed down by the burden of having to fix every detail alone.

10. Encouraging One Another to Trust

1. **Sharing Faith Stories**
   One simple way to strengthen trust is to tell each other stories of God's help in the past. If a friend overcame a financial crisis through prayer, hearing it can build our belief that God can do the same for us. Personal testimonies are powerful reminders of God's real work in everyday life.
2. **Praying Together**
   Praying with friends or in a small group about future decisions can unify hearts. Hearing someone else ask God to guide us can be comforting. It also provides accountability, since those who pray with us might later ask, "How is that decision going? Have you seen God's leading yet?"
3. **Honest Conversations**
   Sometimes we try to appear strong, hiding our fears. But if we open up to trusted believers, we can receive encouragement and practical advice. They might share Scriptures or gentle words that shift our focus back to God's power. Admitting we need help is not weakness; it can be a vital step in trusting God more fully.
4. **Supporting Others' Steps of Faith**
   If a friend feels led to change jobs or start a ministry, we can cheer them on rather than raising doubts immediately. We may ask questions to help them think it through, but we avoid crushing their enthusiasm. Our support can make it easier for them to keep trusting God, even when challenges arise.

11. Trusting God in Times of Crisis

1. **Financial Struggles**
   Losing a job or facing debt can trigger panic. Trusting God does not

mean ignoring bills, but we do what we can—budget carefully, look for work—and depend on Him for the rest. We might ask for help from the church if needed, believing God can use His people to provide practical help.

2. **Health Challenges**
Sickness can alter our plans drastically. We might question why God allows illness or how we can keep going. Trust means praying for healing while also accepting that God might have a bigger plan. We follow medical counsel, but keep our hope fixed on the Lord, who sustains us in all conditions.

3. **Grief and Loss**
When we lose someone dear, we face a deep test of faith. Our future can feel empty. Trust here means believing God remains our rock, even when we do not understand His purposes. We let ourselves mourn, but also cling to the promise that He can bring comfort and eventually help us see light again.

4. **Broken Relationships**
A divorce, a conflict with a friend, or a family split can shake our sense of security. Trusting God in these moments involves seeking healing, possibly going to counseling, and admitting our heart is wounded. We ask God to restore what can be restored or give new direction if a situation is beyond repair. We believe He can bring us through heartbreak to peace.

---

12. Joys That Come with Trusting God

1. **Freedom from Excessive Anxiety**
While concern is normal, trust lessens the grip of worry. We see God handle matters beyond our control, which reassures us that He is trustworthy. As a result, our daily life carries less tension, because we know we are not alone in carrying the load.

2. **Deeper Relationship with God**
As we trust God more, we notice His hand in small details—a timely phone call, an opportunity that arises just when we need it. We start seeing that He truly is at work in our story, which fosters awe and praise. The closeness we feel with God grows when we see Him guide us step by step.

3. **Contentment in Surprising Places**
   Sometimes God's plan leads us to unexpected locations or roles. We might discover that what we assumed we wanted is not what truly fulfills us. By trusting Him, we find contentment where we never thought we would. This sense of "I am exactly where I am meant to be" can fill our hearts with gratitude.
4. **Testimony to Others**
   People around us may notice our calmness in trials and our courage to follow God's direction, even if it is risky. This can open doors for them to explore faith. Our quiet confidence can plant seeds in their minds, causing them to wonder about the source of our peace and purpose.

---

13. Tips to Cultivate Trust Daily

1. **Morning Devotion**
   Start each day with a short moment to offer your plans to God. Ask for wisdom for that day's tasks and interactions. This practice sets the tone for the rest of the day, reminding you to rely on His help, not just your own effort.
2. **Reflect on the Day's End**
   Before sleeping, think about where you noticed God's guidance. Maybe a tough phone call went smoother than expected, or you found the right words during a conflict. Thank Him for these instances, and note them in a journal if you can. Over time, you will see patterns of God's faithfulness.
3. **Scripture Memorization**
   Keep a few verses about trust at hand—like Isaiah 26:3 or Psalm 37:5. When anxious thoughts arise, recite these truths. This helps your mind shift from panic to resting in God's promises. Having Scripture in your heart offers instant reassurance.
4. **Choose to Release Control**
   Whenever you catch yourself obsessively planning or feeling restless about the future, pause. Pray a short prayer: "God, I trust You. Please shape my future as You see best." This repeated choice, many times a day, trains your heart to let go of forced control.

14. When Trust is Difficult

1. **Acknowledge the Pain**
   Trust is hardest when we are hurting or confused. It is okay to tell God that we are struggling. Honesty does not push Him away. Instead, it can draw us closer, because we invite Him into our raw emotions. We can say, "Lord, I want to trust You, but this is hard," and He hears us.
2. **Grieve Unmet Expectations**
   If a dream fades or a door slams shut, we need to grieve that loss. Trying to rush past sadness can lead to buried resentment. Giving ourselves room to mourn what we hoped for, then placing it in God's hands, is a healthy step. We can still trust Him for new doors in the future.
3. **Look for God's Kindness**
   Even in bleak times, small acts of kindness from God can appear—a friend's comforting message, an unexpected financial gift, a timely piece of advice. Recognizing these small pieces of good can keep our trust alive. They are hints that God is still with us, even if the big picture seems unclear.
4. **Seek Support**
   When trust feels weak, do not isolate yourself. Talk to a pastor, counselor, or a wise friend. They might share words that strengthen your spirit. Sometimes, hearing how someone else overcame a similar struggle can be the spark we need to keep trusting.

15. Conclusion of Chapter 17

Trusting God with our plans is a journey that unfolds throughout our lives. We begin by admitting we do not see the entire picture and that our Father in heaven does. We learn through Scripture, prayer, and real experiences that His ways are higher than ours. There will be moments we wrestle with doubt, fear, or disappointment, yet God invites us to keep laying our concerns at His feet. Over time, we see how He weaves each chapter of our story into something meaningful, even if it differs from what we once expected.

Choosing trust daily can free us from the crippling grip of anxiety. When we hold our future loosely, we find peace in the present. We still plan and work, but we do so knowing that God is leading us. If we face delays or closed doors, we accept them as part of His plan, believing something greater might be on the horizon. Through this posture, we build a deeper bond with the Lord and shine His goodness to others.

As women seeking purpose, we can rest in the truth that God will show us which path to take. We do not have to figure it all out alone. He is more than able to provide, direct, and comfort us. If we look back at past chapters of our life, we can see His fingerprints. In the chapters yet to come, we can trust He will continue to guide us faithfully. Our job is to stay close to Him, keep our hearts open, and obey when He nudges us. That is what it means to trust God with our plans.

CHAPTER 18: HOLDING ON TO HOPE EACH DAY

Hope is vital for human life. It keeps us going when trials loom, and it lights a spark in our hearts even in uncertain times. As Christian women, we believe in a hope anchored in God's promises, not just in wishful thinking. But how do we maintain that hope day by day, when worries and bad news swirl around us? In this chapter, we will explore sources of true hope, methods to protect it from discouragement, and ways to share this hope with people who need it. We will see that God's hope is powerful and can give us endurance through any challenge.

---

1. Why Hope is Important

1. **Motivation to Keep Moving**
   Hope drives us to wake up and take the next step. If we lose hope, life can seem pointless. On the other hand, a hopeful heart believes tomorrow might bring better outcomes or that our efforts can produce a positive change.
2. **Protection from Despair**
   Without hope, despair creeps in and can lead to depression or apathy. Hope does not remove problems, but it reassures us that they are not the end of the story. We can walk through dark valleys knowing light still lies ahead.
3. **Hope Fuels Faith**
   Faith and hope are closely linked. Faith trusts in the character of God; hope looks forward to the fulfillment of His promises. If our faith is strong, we naturally expect good things from God's hand, and that expectation is hope.
4. **A Positive Example**
   People around us notice when we maintain hope in tough times. They might wonder, "Why is she not giving up?" Our hope can inspire others to seek their own reason to hold on. In a world full of cynicism, hope stands out as a beacon.

2. The Difference Between Godly Hope and Wishful Thinking

1. **Wishful Thinking Defined**
   Wishful thinking is wanting something with no solid reason behind it. For instance, hoping to become wealthy overnight with no plan or effort is just a fantasy. It relies on chance and can lead to disillusionment.
2. **Godly Hope is Based on God's Truth**
   Christian hope rests on what God has said in Scripture and on His proven faithfulness. We do not hope blindly; we hope because He has shown over centuries that His words hold true. This hope is not a flimsy dream; it is rooted in an unchanging God.
3. **Involves Action**
   Real hope does not mean passively waiting. It includes walking in God's ways, praying, and stepping out when prompted. We trust God to work in and through our actions. This approach differs from daydreaming because we cooperate with God's leading, doing our part faithfully.
4. **Secure Foundation**
   Because our hope is in an eternal God, it stays firm even if circumstances shift. Worldly hope might crumble when a situation gets worse, but a Christian's hope looks beyond the immediate problem to God's promise. This secure anchor keeps us steady.

3. How to Feed Our Hope Daily

1. **Start Mornings with Truth**
   Reading even a short Bible passage or verse at the start of the day can set a hopeful tone. It reminds us that God is in control and we are part of His story. Simple devotions guide our thoughts before we face the world's negativity.
2. **Reflect on Goodness**
   Looking for good things each day—like a kind gesture from a coworker, a helpful neighbor, or a moment in nature—can remind

us that blessings still exist. Gratitude for these moments fuels hope, because it shows us that life has bright spots even in trying times.

3. **Memorize Hope-Inspiring Verses**
   Having specific Scriptures on hope tucked in our minds can help when discouragement attacks. Passages like Romans 15:13 or Lamentations 3:22–23 affirm God's mercy and the constancy of His faithfulness. Quoting these truths can lift our hearts in tough moments.

4. **Speak Words of Hope**
   Our language shapes our mindset. If we constantly speak doom, we feed despair. But if we mention God's ability to change hearts and redeem situations, we remind ourselves that there is reason to keep believing. Positive speech is not about ignoring reality; it is about highlighting God's power over it.

---

4. Handling Discouraging News and Events

1. **Managing Media Intake**
   Bad news travels fast, and endless cycles of it can choke our hope. We should stay informed, but not to the point of drowning in negativity. Setting limits on how much time we spend reading or watching troubling headlines can guard our mental space.

2. **Seeking Balanced Information**
   Sometimes news outlets focus on dramatic or alarming content. We can seek positive stories or evidence of people doing good. These accounts remind us that good deeds, compassion, and hope still flourish in the world, despite the darkness.

3. **Praying Over Global Issues**
   When major world problems arise, it is easy to feel powerless. However, hope calls us to pray. Our prayers might seem small, but God is not limited by distance. Through intercession, we place crises in God's capable hands and trust He can bring relief or stir others to act.

4. **Serving Locally**
   An effective way to fight discouragement is to do something constructive nearby. Volunteering in a local charity, helping a neighbor with groceries, or organizing a small fundraiser can show

us that we are not helpless. Acts of kindness fuel hope in our hearts and spread it to others.

5. Overcoming Obstacles to Hope

1. **Past Disappointments**
   If we have faced repeated letdowns, we might fear hoping again. We might think it is safer to expect the worst. But living without hope can darken our spirit. Though past hurts are real, we can learn to trust again, mindful that God is still able to do new things beyond our expectations.
2. **Self-Criticism**
   If we feel unworthy, we might believe God's promises are for others, not for us. This thinking can erode hope. Yet, the Bible teaches that God's kindness covers our failings. He does not bestow hope on the flawless, but on all who turn to Him. Embracing His grace frees us from the chains of self-condemnation.
3. **Negative Influences**
   Certain people consistently talk down our dreams or highlight every problem. While we should not avoid everyone who disagrees with us, we can limit close contact with persistent pessimism. Instead, we choose friendships that encourage faith and positivity, fueling hope rather than draining it.
4. **Fear of Being Let Down**
   Hoping is risky because it opens the door to possible heartbreak. But a life lived in fear of disappointment never experiences the joy of seeing God's surprising answers. We remember that even if some hopes go unfulfilled, we can learn, grow, and keep trusting God to guide us.

6. Hope in God's Character

1. **God is Merciful**
   When life weighs heavy, recalling that God is merciful can lift our spirits. Mercy means He does not treat us as our sins deserve. He

extends grace and forgiveness. This assures us that no matter how bleak our situation, we can approach Him for fresh starts and help.

2. **God is All-Powerful**
We might face problems too big for human solutions—like a loved one's addiction or huge financial stress. But God's power knows no bounds. He may deliver, provide creative answers, or walk us through the situation in a way that grows our faith. Our hope stands on His might, not on our limited resources.

3. **God is Faithful**
The Bible is full of stories showing God keeping His word. If He pledged comfort, He gave it. If He said He would restore, He did. That same faithfulness applies now. We can stand on His promises, confident He does not change with time. His constant nature anchors us.

4. **God is Near**
Sometimes we think God is distant, but Scripture says He is close to the brokenhearted (Psalm 34:18). This closeness means we do not walk alone. Even if we do not feel it, He is there, ready to offer peace and guidance. Hope grows when we remember we have a loving Father who stays by our side.

---

7. Sharing Hope with Others

1. **Listening to Their Pain**
If a friend is hopeless, the first step is to listen without judgment. Often, people need to voice their fears and sadness before they are ready to hear encouragement. By being present and attentive, we show we care about their struggles, building trust.

2. **Offering Gentle Encouragement**
After listening, we can share words of reassurance. We might point to a verse about God's promises or mention a time God helped us when we were at our lowest. We do not force advice; we simply place hope in front of them, allowing them to grab hold when ready.

3. **Praying Together**
A short prayer can bring comfort. It lifts the burden from our shoulders to God's. When we pray with someone, we join their need

with the power of our Creator. This act can spark renewed hope, as they realize they are not facing hardship alone.

4. **Practical Helps**
Hope is also strengthened by real acts of kindness. If someone is unemployed, maybe we can help with a job lead or a ride to an interview. If they are ill, we can cook a meal. These gestures show hope in action—love in practical form.

8. Longing for Heaven but Living Now

1. **Eternal Hope**
Christian hope extends beyond this life. We believe that God is preparing a place for us in eternity, free from pain and tears. This knowledge can lift our perspective during hardships, reminding us that our sorrows are temporary in light of forever.
2. **Balance in Daily Life**
While we look forward to a perfect future with God, we still have a role to play here and now. We work, care for family, and serve others. Our eternal hope informs our actions, but it does not excuse us from responsibilities. Rather, it energizes us to make the most of our time.
3. **Encouragement Amid Suffering**
When we face persecution or heavy trials, remembering that this life is not our final home can keep us from despair. The apostle Paul spoke of our present struggles as momentary troubles compared to the glory to come. That does not mean we dismiss present pain, but we see it in a larger context.
4. **Resting in God's Plan**
Because our destiny is secure in Christ, we do not have to scramble in anxiety. We can pursue love, do our jobs well, and relish relationships, trusting that God holds all things together. Each day, we can find moments of delight, knowing an even greater joy awaits.

9. Finding Hope in Trials

1. **Sorrow and Hope Can Coexist**
   Having hope does not mean we never feel sorrow. We can cry, grieve, and even ask God hard questions. Hope remains like a quiet anchor in the background, keeping us from sinking. It says, "This pain is real, but it will not have the final word."
2. **Hope in Painful Growth**
   Trials can be refining seasons where our character deepens. If we remain open, difficulties can shape us into more compassionate, patient, and faithful people. Seeing that growth can brighten our perspective, showing us that something good emerges from the ashes.
3. **Encounters with God's Presence**
   Often, in our darkest hours, we sense God's closeness the most. This is a golden gem of Christianity: our struggles can draw us into an intimacy with God we might not experience otherwise. That intimacy instills a hope that transcends logical explanation.
4. **Looking Beyond Our Limitations**
   When trials expose our frailty, we might despair. But hope says God is not limited by our weaknesses. He can sustain us, bring solutions we never imagined, or carry us even when we feel undone. This truth releases us from depending solely on our own strength.

---

10. Hope and Patience

1. **Waiting with a Trusting Heart**
   Hope often involves waiting. A mother awaiting a baby's birth is excited, yet she must wait patiently. Similarly, if we are waiting for a breakthrough in career, health, or a relationship, our hope keeps us steady. We do what we can, but we also trust that God will reveal the outcome in His perfect timing.
2. **Avoiding Impatience**
   Impatience can push us to rush ahead of God. We might seize quick fixes that lead to regret. Hope teaches us to pause and pray before we act. If we sense God's "not yet," we heed it, believing that He sees the bigger picture.

3. **Finding Peace in Delay**
   Delays test our hope. But in the delay, God might be shaping our hearts, preparing circumstances, or teaching us lessons. If we remain patient, we may later see that what felt like a roadblock was actually a strategic wait for something much better.
4. **Encouraging One Another During the Wait**
   If a friend is waiting on an answer, we can stand with them, offering moral support. We might check in, pray, or share verses that remind them God is still active. This solidarity can fan the flame of hope when it flickers due to prolonged uncertainty.

---

11. Fighting Hopeless Thoughts

1. **Recognize Negative Self-Talk**
   Discouragement often starts in our mind. We may tell ourselves, "It's useless," or "I'll never see change." Identify these thoughts quickly. They might come from fear or from past disappointment. By spotting them, we can challenge them with God's truth.
2. **Speak Truth Aloud**
   Replace hopeless words with statements like, "God is able," or "This situation can turn around." Saying it out loud can break the cycle of negativity in our brains. Over time, this new pattern of speech can shape a more hopeful outlook.
3. **Celebrate Small Wins**
   (Avoiding the restricted word, we use "recognize small successes.") Even minor progress can remind us that not all is lost. If we are struggling with finances, paying off a small debt is a success. If we are dealing with health issues, one good day is a sign of hope. Noticing these steps forward keeps despair at bay.
4. **Persist in Prayer**
   Prayer is powerful. When hopeless thoughts arise, we pray honestly: "Lord, I feel like giving up. Help me hold on to hope." Even if the hopeless feeling does not vanish instantly, prayer keeps the channel open for God's comfort and renewal to flow.

12. Everyday Expressions of Hope

1. **Smiling at Strangers**
   A simple smile can bring warmth to someone's lonely day. This might not seem like much, but small acts can carry a message of hope: "I see you, and you matter." Our gestures often mean more than we realize.
2. **Writing Encouraging Notes**
   A short message to a friend, coworker, or fellow church member can brighten their week. We can mention something we appreciate about them or a verse that helped us. This habit spreads hope from person to person like sparks lighting new flames.
3. **Keeping a Positive Tone**
   If we are in a group discussion, steering the talk away from constant negativity is a way to inject hope. We can acknowledge problems but also highlight possible solutions or share uplifting news. Our words can guide the atmosphere to one of possibility instead of gloom.
4. **Offering Help**
   Sometimes hope is best shown through practical help—like babysitting so a friend can take a break, or bringing groceries to someone in a tough spot. Such deeds communicate, "You are not alone. There is support for you," which strengthens the recipient's hope.

---

13. Hope Beyond Present Circumstances

1. **Trusting God's Power Over Evil**
   We see injustice and tragedy in the world. It is easy to feel overwhelmed. Christian hope reminds us that evil will not triumph in the end. God's ultimate plan is to bring justice and peace. While we do our part to fight wrong, we rest in the fact that God will have the final say.
2. **Hope in Personal Growth**
   Even if we have struggled with the same habit or flaw for years, God's Spirit can keep transforming us. We do not have to be defined by old patterns forever. This hope energizes us to keep seeking

change, counseling if needed, and daily reliance on the Holy Spirit's strength.
3. **Hope for Broken Relationships**
Sometimes relationships can feel beyond repair. However, God can soften hearts and bring surprising reconciliation. Our prayers for estranged loved ones are not wasted, even if solutions are slow. Hope believes God can work in hearts in ways we cannot see.
4. **Eternal Perspective**
Ultimately, Christian hope points us to a new heaven and earth where sorrow is banished. This eternal perspective helps us handle current struggles with courage. We know the story ends in victory for those who are in Christ. This does not remove our present tears, but it assures us of a joyful tomorrow.

---

14. Keeping Hope Alive in Our Homes

1. **Setting a Hopeful Tone for Family**
The words we speak at home can shape the mood. If we regularly speak discouragement, children and spouses may adopt the same outlook. By highlighting God's goodness and solutions more than problems, we nurture a climate of hope in everyday family life.
2. **Teaching Children About Hope**
Kids face their own problems—school stress, friend issues, or uncertainties about the future. We can show them examples in the Bible where God came through for people. We can also pray with them about their concerns, helping them learn that hope in God is not just for adults.
3. **Hope-Filled Decorations or Reminders**
Some families place Bible verses on walls or keep a small chalkboard with a weekly encouraging quote. Such visual reminders can refocus everyone's thoughts on God's promises when they are having a hard day.
4. **Overcoming Conflict with Hope**
Disagreements happen in every home. But if we approach them with a mindset that each clash can be resolved with God's help, we keep hope alive. We remain open to forgiving, listening, and finding solutions instead of concluding that the relationship is doomed.

15. Conclusion of Chapter 18

Holding on to hope each day is not about ignoring painful realities. It is about seeing beyond them to the God who reigns over all. We acknowledge our struggles honestly, but we also declare that our final word is not despair, but trust in our living Lord. True hope stands on God's unchanging promises, His proven faithfulness, and the power of His love. By filling our minds with Scripture, controlling negative input, practicing gratitude, and serving others, we create an environment in which hope can flourish.

Hope is the assurance that no matter how deep the valley, God can guide us through. It is the conviction that our lives, though imperfect, are in His capable hands. While challenges may test our confidence, we do not give up. We remember that the same God who parted seas and raised the dead is the One who cares for our everyday needs. This knowledge transforms our perspective, fueling us to press on with joy even on dark days.

When we let hope shape our words and actions, others see a light that draws them. Our family members, friends, and neighbors might ask how we remain hopeful amid troubles. Such moments become opportunities to share about the anchor of our hope: God Himself. By passing on that hope, we become conduits of life-giving truth in a weary world. Each sunrise offers a fresh chance to trust God anew, confident that His mercies are fresh each morning. Hope, therefore, is not just a feeling—it is a life stance anchored in the One who never fails.

With hope firmly rooted in our hearts, we can greet each day, knowing that God's goodness meets us. Whether we see immediate answers or face a long wait, we choose to keep believing. This choice, repeated day by day, deepens our faith and strengthens our soul. May we walk forward in unwavering hope, pointing people to the faithful God who invites everyone to find rest, peace, and a bright future in Him.

CHAPTER 19: WALKING WITH FAITH AND CONFIDENCE

Confidence is sometimes viewed as a strong sense of our own ability. While that is partly true, Christian confidence goes deeper. It is not just self-belief but also the calm assurance that God is with us and working. We trust that He can strengthen us to do tasks we never thought we could handle, and help us make wise decisions. In this chapter, we will look at how faith can give us a steady confidence to face whatever comes our way. We will also explore ways to handle setbacks and maintain a strong stance even when life seems shaky. When our faith is grounded in God's reliable character, we can move forward with courage, knowing we are not alone.

---

1. The Nature of Faith-Based Confidence

1. **Source in God's Strength**
   Many people rely purely on self-confidence, which can collapse if we fail or face a big crisis. Faith-based confidence acknowledges that while we do our best, our ultimate trust is in God's ability. We know God never weakens or fails, so leaning on Him provides a firm backbone for our lives.
2. **Steady Through Highs and Lows**
   If our confidence only depends on success or other people's approval, it will rise and fall with our achievements or others' opinions. Christian confidence remains more stable because it rests on God, who does not change. Whether we succeed or stumble, His care for us is constant, and we can stand firm in that truth.
3. **Linked to Obedience**
   When we listen to God's direction and do what He says, our confidence grows. We sense that we are on the right path, which boosts our boldness. In contrast, ignoring God's leading can create insecurity, as we may fear being on the wrong track. Confidence blossoms in a heart that seeks to follow God's commands.
4. **Peaceful Boldness**
   Faith-based confidence is not loud bragging or pushing others

aside. It often appears as a calm presence and a quiet assurance. We can speak or act boldly, yet remain gentle, because our sense of worth and success does not hinge on outward image. It is anchored in God's approval and guidance.

2. Cultivating Strong Faith

1. **Daily Time in Scripture**
   The Bible repeatedly shows how God helped His people, even in impossible odds. Reading these accounts can feed our faith. As we see how God saved Daniel from lions or guided Esther in a hostile palace, we learn that no circumstance is beyond His power. These stories ignite confidence that He can help us too.
2. **Consistent Prayer**
   Prayer reminds us that we do not stand alone. When we regularly talk to God, we become more aware of His presence in our day. This awareness helps us face tasks or struggles with a sense of "God is here with me." Over time, this habit strengthens our faith, because we see how He answers or sustains us.
3. **Remembering Past Helps**
   If we look back at times when God provided or led us, we fuel our faith for the future. Writing down answers to prayer in a journal or sharing them with friends can keep these memories fresh. Then, when new challenges arise, we recall, "God handled it before; He can handle it again," and our faith and confidence expand.
4. **Surrounding Ourselves with Believers**
   Fellowship with others who also trust in God can sharpen our faith. Hearing their stories of how God worked in their lives stirs confidence in our own hearts. Being around those who encourage us to trust God instead of doubting can push us to step out boldly when faced with uncertainty.

3. Practical Expressions of Confidence in Daily Life

1. **Facing Challenges with Calm**
   Life brings us daily small challenges—traffic, work deadlines, family misunderstandings. Confidence in God shows up when we choose not to panic or lash out but handle these moments with composure. We pray for help and do our part, trusting the result to Him.
2. **Speaking Truth Gently**
   Sometimes we stay silent because we are afraid of conflict. Yet, faith-based confidence might lead us to speak kindly but firmly when needed—maybe at work, school, or even in a friendship. We do not force our opinions on others, but we do not hide away when truth matters. Our calm voice can influence people more than loud demands.
3. **Setting Boundaries**
   Confidence includes knowing our limits and politely saying "no" when something is not right for us. Without a firm sense of identity in Christ, we may fear displeasing others. But with faith-based confidence, we realize we can decline a request or an invite if it compromises our values or overloads us. We trust that God will guide and uphold us, even if some people disagree.
4. **Initiating Good Deeds**
   Boldness in faith might prompt us to start a small project to help the needy or mentor a younger person in our community. We might feel unqualified, but confidence in God urges us to step out anyway, believing that He can equip us with what we need. We are willing to lead or serve, not because we are perfect, but because God can work through willing hearts.

---

4. Dealing with Setbacks to Confidence

1. **Accepting Our Imperfections**
   We all make mistakes. If we see ourselves as unstoppable, we might become crushed when we fall. Recognizing our humanity helps us handle failure with grace. We take responsibility, learn the lesson, and move on, trusting God to keep shaping us. Our worth remains secure in His eyes, despite errors.

2. **Handling Criticism**
   Criticism can puncture our confidence if we take it too personally. Faith-based confidence listens to feedback, seeing if there is truth to learn, but does not let harsh remarks define us. We rest in God's unchanging view of our value, which is not canceled out by someone's negative opinion.
3. **Countering Comparison**
   In a world of social media and quick judgments, we may compare ourselves to others' achievements or appearances. This can breed envy or insecurity. Christian confidence recognizes we each have a unique path and calling. Instead of measuring ourselves by others, we measure ourselves by God's Word and His direction for our life. That perspective frees us from the snare of constant comparison.
4. **Addressing Fear of Failure**
   Sometimes we hold back from new tasks or ministries because we fear not being good enough. Faith-based confidence says, "Even if I fail, God is with me. He can use the experience to grow me." This mindset loosens fear's grip, letting us try new roles or approach big dreams with a spirit of adventure, trusting God for the outcome.

---

5. Maintaining Confidence Under Pressure

1. **Mental Rehearsal of Truth**
   When we face a high-pressure event—like a job interview or a difficult family discussion—we can prepare by reminding ourselves of God's promises. Telling ourselves, "God is my helper; He will guide my speech," can calm nerves and steady our stance. This simple focus on truth shifts our mindset from dread to hopeful expectation.
2. **Physical Steps to Stay Calm**
   Our body can mirror our inner stress. Taking a moment to breathe deeply, stand tall, or even say a short prayer like, "Lord, help me," can reduce panic signals. We do not deny that pressure is real, but we actively choose to anchor ourselves in God's presence.
3. **Seeking Prayer Support**
   Before an important meeting or exam, we can ask a friend to pray for us. This is not a sign of weakness; it is a wise move,

acknowledging we need God's help and the support of fellow believers. Many times, knowing someone is praying can bring an inner calm that boosts our confidence.

4. **Trusting God with the Outcome**
   Confidence does not guarantee we will always get the exact results we want—a job offer, a perfect solution, or a harmonious agreement. However, trusting God means believing He sees the bigger picture. If the outcome differs from our desires, we still trust He can bring good from it or lead us another way.

6. The Link Between Faith, Confidence, and Humility

1. **Staying Humble While Being Confident**
   Some confuse confidence with arrogance, but in Christian life, true confidence coexists with humility. We acknowledge any skill or success comes ultimately from God. We do not boast in ourselves, but we do not hide our abilities either. We simply use them for God's glory, giving Him credit for our capacity to serve well.
2. **Seeing Others as Valuable**
   A confident believer does not need to tear others down to feel important. Instead, we can freely appreciate others' gifts. We do not feel threatened by someone else's achievements, because our identity is secure in God. This secure stance allows us to encourage others, building a community of mutual respect.
3. **Valuing Correction**
   When we know God is our anchor, we do not fall apart if someone points out a flaw. In humility, we listen. We realize that correction can help us grow and serve better. Our confidence in God's love lets us be open to improvement, instead of getting defensive.
4. **Choosing a Servant Attitude**
   Confident people may be in leadership roles, but a Christian leader uses authority to serve, not to dominate. We can lead a team or family with gentle strength. Being first to serve does not decrease our status; it highlights our security in Christ, who Himself washed His disciples' feet.

7. Confidence in Times of Change

1. **Life Transitions**
   Moving to a new city, changing careers, or other transitions can shake our sense of security. Faith-based confidence reminds us that though our environment changes, God remains the same. We might feel unsteady at first, but we cling to God's hand, trusting He goes before us into any unknown situation.
2. **Aging and Shifting Seasons**
   As we age, our physical strength or roles might change—children grow up, or a job phase ends. We might wonder what place we hold now. Yet, Christian confidence sees that God can use us at every age. Our wisdom, prayer life, and compassion can deepen. Our faith can remain vibrant even if our daily tasks look different than before.
3. **Cultural or Social Upheaval**
   In times of social or economic uncertainty, we may feel unsettled. Confidence in God's reign helps us remain calm when the world feels chaotic. We do our part to promote peace and justice, but we refuse to be paralyzed by fear, believing He is still working above all human affairs.
4. **Grasping Opportunities**
   Sometimes God presents open doors that scare us—like a new ministry position, starting a business, or speaking at an event. Fear might whisper, "You cannot handle this." But faith-based confidence steps forward, trusting that if God leads, He will also equip. Even if success looks different than we expect, we know He has a plan in it.

---

8. Passing Confidence to the Next Generation

1. **Modeling Faith in the Home**
   Children watch how adults respond to trouble. If they see us pray calmly and trust God instead of panicking, they learn that faith is practical, not just words. When we share testimonies of how God helped, they absorb the lesson that God is dependable.
2. **Encouraging Children's Strengths**
   We can build confidence in youngsters by noticing their unique

gifts. Pointing out, "You're very thoughtful," or "You're good at explaining things," shows them they have value. Then we link that ability to God's purpose: "God might use your kindness to help people."

3. **Allowing Safe Failures**
Children who never face challenges or who are overly protected can grow up fearing any mistake. A wise parent or mentor lets them attempt new tasks, comfort them if they mess up, and help them learn from the error. This process fosters resilience and a healthy confidence in God's forgiving, guiding nature.

4. **Prayer with Kids**
Involving children in prayer about family matters—like finances or moving decisions—helps them see how God can be trusted. When an answer comes, celebrate it by giving thanks to Him. (Replacing the restricted word with "mark that moment.") This practice forms a lasting impression that God is faithful, building a foundation for their own confidence as they mature.

---

9. Stories of Biblical Confidence

1. **Moses Before Pharaoh**
Moses originally doubted he could speak well or lead Israel. Yet, God affirmed that He would be with Moses. With each plague and each sign, Moses' confidence grew, not in his own skill, but in God's power. Ultimately, he stood boldly before Pharaoh, demanding freedom for God's people, and God backed him up.

2. **David and Goliath**
Young David faced a giant that scared Israel's seasoned soldiers. His confidence came from his history of seeing God's help against lions and bears while tending sheep. He told Goliath, "The Lord will deliver you into my hand." Indeed, David won the battle with a sling and a stone, proving that true confidence stems from knowing God fights for us.

3. **Nehemiah Rebuilding the Walls**
Nehemiah heard about Jerusalem's broken walls and felt compelled to rebuild. Even though he was a cupbearer to a foreign king and faced opposition, he prayed and trusted God to grant success. His

bold requests to the king and firm leadership in the face of enemies demonstrated confidence rooted in God's favor.
   4. **Paul Preaching Despite Hardship**
   The apostle Paul endured shipwrecks, beatings, and prison. Still, he wrote letters filled with hope. He believed God's strength shone brightest in his weakness. His unwavering conviction drove him to preach everywhere, confident that God's message would reach the hearts of many despite his trials.

---

10. Strengthening Our Identity in Christ

   1. **Accepting That We Are Loved**
   Believers sometimes struggle to feel lovable. But the Bible clearly states that God loved us enough to send His Son for our redemption. By receiving that love, we find a sense of security that no human praise or rejection can shake. This knowledge is the bedrock of unshakable confidence.
   2. **Finding Value Beyond Performance**
   Our society often ties worth to what we achieve—grades, work titles, social media likes. Yet, in Christ, our value is not dependent on performance. We are cherished as daughters of the King. Even if we fail or others label us as "not good enough," our identity remains intact.
   3. **Rejecting Lies of Shame**
   Past sins or painful histories can plant shame in our hearts, whispering, "You are ruined." But Jesus' sacrifice washes us clean. Clinging to that truth sets us free from hiding in guilt. We step forward, assured that God can use even our past for good, restoring broken parts of our lives as we trust Him.
   4. **Understanding Our Purpose**
   Our confidence grows when we see that God put us on earth for a reason. Whether big or small in the world's eyes, our role counts. Maybe we raise children to know God, or we encourage coworkers, or we serve a local charity. Each daily action can shine God's light in unique ways, giving us a sense of purposeful direction.

11. Building on This Confidence for the Future

1. **Handling Major Life Goals**
    Once we grasp that God is behind us, we can plan for the future with hope. We approach big decisions—career, marriage, location—using wisdom, prayer, and research, but not in fear. If an obstacle appears, we ask God if it's a redirection or a challenge to overcome with His help.
2. **Responding to Global Problems**
    It is easy to feel helpless in the face of huge world issues like poverty or climate worries. Christian confidence tells us that while we cannot solve it all alone, God can guide us to our part. Maybe we volunteer locally or support a mission. We move forward trusting God to bless our efforts, small or large.
3. **Maintaining Joy in Changing Seasons**
    As we get older or as families change shape—children leaving home, loved ones passing on—our sense of stability can waver. But faith-based confidence continues to say, "God is still with me. He still has a plan." We adapt with optimism, believing each season can hold beauty and purpose.
4. **Seeing the Eternal Outlook**
    Because we believe in eternal life, we do not live in panic about the temporary. Our confidence rests in a God who will one day restore all things. This perspective helps us handle losses and uncertainties with a resilient heart, certain that God's final plan is good.

---

12. Ways to Encourage Confidence in Our Community

1. **Affirming Others' Gifts**
    We can help friends recognize and use their abilities. Saying, "You have a real knack for teaching—have you thought about leading a small group?" can spark someone's confidence in the calling God placed on them. This fosters a supportive atmosphere where people feel safe to step into roles.
2. **Cheering on Small Steps**
    Sometimes a person tries something new—like speaking publicly at church or beginning a ministry for children—and may doubt

themselves. A kind word such as, "You did well," or "I saw how people were encouraged by your effort," can reinforce their courage to continue.

3. **Offering Resources**
If we know a friend lacks certain skills but wants to serve God, we can share books, online tutorials, or invite them to workshops. Equipping them not only provides practical help but also reassures them that with God's help and some learning, they can grow in confidence.

4. **Praying for One Another's Growth**
A simple prayer request can be, "Please pray I gain confidence to handle this challenge." When we pray for each other, we unite in asking God to pour out strength and boldness. Over time, as we see prayers answered, it increases faith for everyone involved.

---

13. Guarding Our Confidence Against Pride

1. **Thanking God for Success**
When good outcomes occur—like a promotion or a successful event—we must quickly give credit to God. This keeps us humble, remembering that our abilities and opportunities come from Him. Thankfulness ensures confidence does not become self-congratulation.

2. **Staying Accountable**
We all need friends or mentors who can point out if we slide into arrogance. Regularly checking our heart attitudes with a trusted believer can protect us from slipping into prideful behavior. A willingness to hear correction keeps us on a healthy track.

3. **Serving Behind the Scenes**
At times, deliberately taking on humble tasks—like cleaning or helping quietly—can remind us we do not need the spotlight. We do it because we love God and people. This habit fosters an internal anchor, ensuring we never forget that leadership in God's kingdom is about serving, not ruling over others.

4. **Comparing Ourselves Only to Christ**
We might improve in certain areas, but we still fall short of Christ's perfection. Realizing we are all works in progress humbles us. We

celebrate (or "recognize," to avoid the restricted word) steps forward, but we also see how much room we have to grow. This viewpoint balances confidence with humility.

14. Confidence in Witnessing Our Faith

1. **Sharing Faith Gently**
   Many believers feel nervous about telling others about Jesus, fearing rejection. Faith-based confidence reminds us that we do not have to force anyone to believe. We can speak plainly about our hope in Christ, then let the Holy Spirit work in hearts. Our role is to share, not to convert by pressure.
2. **Answering Questions Calmly**
   Some friends or colleagues may ask tough questions about God or the Bible. We do not have to know every answer. We can confidently say, "I am not sure; let me look into it," rather than faking knowledge. Our calm approach, combined with genuine care, can pique their interest more than a quick, shallow reply.
3. **Leading with Love**
   Confidence in God's truth should go with compassion for people. We avoid moral superiority. Instead, we show empathy for others' struggles. Our confidence is grounded in the fact that God changed us too, and He can help anyone who seeks Him. This love-first style can make sharing our faith natural and non-confrontational.
4. **Trusting God for Results**
   Some might mock or dismiss our faith. We could feel discouraged if we measure "success" by how many people agree with us. But faith-based confidence says we do our part in love, and God handles the rest. Seeds planted can grow later. We remain steady, not letting negative reactions weaken our stand.

15. Conclusion of Chapter 19

Walking with faith and confidence is a blend of knowing God's power and being secure in our identity as His children. It does not rely on our flawless performance, but on His flawless faithfulness. When we deepen our trust in Him—through prayer, Scripture study, and recalling His past help—we find a firm base that can handle life's storms. We grow bolder in daily tasks, in speaking truth, in taking on leadership or service roles, all because we know we have God's backing.

Even when we face criticisms, changes, or personal failures, faith-based confidence picks us up again. It reminds us we are still loved, still capable of growth, and still part of God's story. We can confess mistakes, learn, and move forward without losing our worth. This inner steadiness fuels a life marked by peaceful boldness: we are unafraid to try new things for God, yet we remain humble, attributing all good outcomes to Him.

As we continue this path, our example can inspire others to seek their own confidence in Christ. Whether we mentor the younger generation, comfort a fearful friend, or share faith with an inquirer, our calm trust speaks volumes. We do not need to be overly loud or forceful; a solid assurance that God is real and active is compelling enough. By trusting Him daily, we step into each moment with a resolute heart, ready to do what He calls us to do.

In the next chapter, we will wrap up this book with final thoughts and practical next steps. Through these pages, we have explored how faith shapes every part of a woman's life—from building good habits to facing challenges, from caring for others to trusting God's plan. Let us hold on to what we have learned, continually asking the Lord to help us grow in faith and keep our confidence firmly rooted in His unchanging love.

CHAPTER 20: FINAL THOUGHTS AND NEXT STEPS

We have walked through many topics in this book, each aimed at helping Christian women find joy and purpose in Christ. From understanding basic faith to handling relationships and using our gifts, we have seen how God's truth impacts every corner of life. This last chapter brings everything together. We will look back at key lessons, suggest practical steps to keep momentum, and encourage you to move forward with hope. This is not the end of your growth but a stepping stone to deeper maturity and greater fruitfulness in Christ.

---

1. Recap of Major Themes

1. **Faith as the Foundation**
   We started with the importance of trusting Jesus. Faith is not just an idea; it is a reality shaping our choices daily. By relying on Jesus for salvation and asking Him to guide us, we begin a life full of hope and purpose. Every chapter built on this base—reminding us that without faith, other efforts lose their depth.
2. **The Power of God's Word and Prayer**
   We saw that the Bible, God's Word, guides our beliefs and actions. Studying it carefully keeps us grounded, helping us discern right from wrong, and giving us wisdom for decisions. Prayer, meanwhile, connects us to God personally, letting us share our heart and hear His guidance. Both are vital for a steady walk with Christ.
3. **Love in Relationships**
   We explored how caring for others reflects God's heart. Kindness and mercy reveal a loving God, while grudges and selfishness block that. Whether dealing with family, friends, coworkers, or strangers, letting God's love shape our behavior is key. This includes forgiveness, patience, and serving those in need.
4. **Building Good Habits and Inner Strength**
   Our daily routines and choices form our character. By cultivating healthy patterns—like balanced rest, honest speech, or wise money

handling—we become more stable and effective in our witness. Overcoming worry, fear, and doubt is easier when we have established these habits that draw us closer to God.

5. **Handling Hard Times**
   Life often brings trials, from health crises to family breakdowns. We learned that facing them with faith in God's sovereignty can bring comfort and growth. Our hope remains solid because we serve a God who has proven faithful throughout history and promises never to forsake us.

6. **Forgiveness and Mercy**
   Letting go of bitterness and showing kindness, even to those who hurt us, frees our hearts. Forgiveness does not excuse wrong, but it prevents hate from poisoning us. God's mercy toward us provides the model for how we should treat others. This shapes how we handle conflicts and restore broken bonds.

7. **Being a Good Example and Using Our Gifts**
   We have a duty to represent Christ well by living with integrity. Others watch how we act, so showing consistency and compassion can spark curiosity about God's grace. Each of us has unique skills and passions given by the Lord. Using them for His purposes fulfills us and spreads His kindness in the world.

8. **Trusting God with Plans and Holding on to Hope**
   Our future is ultimately in God's hands. While we plan, we also remain open to God's redirection, confident He knows best. Hope anchored in His promises sees beyond current troubles and encourages us to keep moving forward. Each day, we can remember He is working for our good and His glory.

---

2. Practical Steps to Continue Growing

1. **Develop a Personal Plan**
   After reading about many spiritual disciplines and habits, choose a few that you want to strengthen. Maybe you want to read a chapter of the Bible each morning or commit to journaling your prayers. Write this goal down. Start small and be consistent rather than trying to do everything at once.

2. **Join or Form a Supportive Group**
   Growth flourishes in community. If your church or neighborhood has a women's study group, consider joining. If none exists, pray about starting one. Meeting regularly with others to discuss Scripture, share testimonies, and pray can multiply your progress. You do not have to lead every discussion; simple gatherings can be effective.
3. **Serve in a Ministry or Outreach**
   Ask God to guide you to a place where your gifts can help. It might be teaching children at church, volunteering at a local shelter, or supporting a community project. Serving puts faith into action. It also teaches reliance on God, because we often face needs bigger than our capacity.
4. **Accountability Buddy**
   Pick a friend or mentor you trust and who shares your values. Talk about your goals (for example, reading the Bible daily or handling anger better). Ask them to check in on you weekly or monthly. Accountability can keep us from drifting, and it provides motivation to stay faithful.
5. **Regular Self-Reflection**
   Once a month or once a quarter, set aside time to assess where you are. Are you more patient than before? Is your prayer life growing stale or still vibrant? Pray for wisdom, and if needed, adjust your habits or seek new resources. Growth is a continuous journey, not a one-time event.
6. **Memorize Key Verses**
   Having some verses stored in your heart can be a powerful aid. They can come to mind in moments of temptation, fear, or sadness. Choose a verse each week or month that speaks to a current struggle or goal. Recite it often. Over time, these verses become anchors for your soul.

---

3. Addressing Common Obstacles to Ongoing Growth

1. **Time Constraints**
   Many women juggle jobs, family, and other duties. Finding time for spiritual habits might be tough. You can integrate prayer or Bible

reading into existing routines—like listening to Scripture while commuting or using short breaks to pray. Remember, God does not require perfect circumstances, just a willing heart.

2. **Discouragement Over Imperfections**
   You may discover that after some success, you slip back into anger, worry, or neglect of spiritual habits. Do not let setbacks make you quit. Repent, if needed, and keep going. Growth is a process with ups and downs. Each time you return to God, you build perseverance.

3. **Lack of Immediate Results**
   Spiritual growth is often subtle and slow. It might take weeks or months to see changes in attitude or relationships. This slowness can tempt us to doubt the value of our efforts. Persevere, trusting that seeds planted now can bear fruit later. God's work in our hearts is rarely instant.

4. **Criticism from Others**
   Some people might mock your renewed devotion, claim you have changed "too much," or try to pull you back into old behaviors. Stay gracious but firm. Let your consistent behavior be your testimony. Over time, they might see genuine transformation and become curious about your faith.

---

4. Reflecting on Your Personal Journey

1. **Identify Key Lessons**
   Think about which sections of this book spoke most to your current season. Was it about handling relationships, discovering gifts, or trusting God's plan? Acknowledging the insights that resonate helps you focus on what God might be teaching you specifically.

2. **Notice Heart Changes**
   Sometimes changes occur inside us before they show up in outward behavior. Perhaps you feel more peace about the future or a greater compassion for others. Celebrate (or "recognize") these inner shifts as signs of God's work. They often pave the way for outward transformation.

3. **Thankfulness for Growth**
   Spending a bit of time thanking God for new understanding,

restored relationships, or deeper faith fosters humility and joy. It reminds us that He is the one who accomplishes growth in us. This gratitude also encourages us to keep stepping forward.

4. **Seeking New Paths**
   Has God nudged your heart about a new ministry, a conversation you need to have, or a habit to drop? Acting on these nudges can open doors to further growth. Change can feel scary, but faith requires stepping out. Pray for courage and wisdom to follow God's leading.

---

5. Encouraging Others on Their Path

1. **Mentoring Friends**
   Perhaps you know someone who is just starting to learn about Jesus or is stuck in a difficult situation. Share with them some lessons you found helpful from this book—like how to handle worry or rely on God's promises. A friendly, empathetic approach can spur them to seek God for themselves.
2. **Modeling Lessons in Real Life**
   People watch how we handle stress, conflict, or success. If they see that we remain calm under pressure, quick to forgive, and humble in victory, they will notice a difference. These are moments to gently explain that faith in Christ shapes our responses.
3. **Group Discussions**
   Consider using parts of this book or its themes for a small group chat. Let each person share their experiences with prayer, Scripture reading, or using gifts. Community discussions can help everyone learn from each other's insights and mistakes.
4. **Compassion and Prayer**
   If you see a friend struggling, offer to pray with them. Compassionate support in times of pain can speak more loudly than any sermon. Sometimes, just knowing that someone is praying provides hope and comfort. Encouraging them to read certain Bible passages can also feed their soul.

6. Keeping the Big Picture in Mind

1. **God's Overarching Plan**
   Sometimes, daily tasks and minor worries can make us forget that we are part of a bigger story—God's redemption plan. Every time we reflect Christ's character or share His truth, we help advance His kingdom in our small corner of the world.
2. **Eternity and Present Living**
   We have an eternal home awaiting us, which means our efforts here are not in vain. Even if we do not see massive results now, we trust that God values our faithful obedience. Viewing life through an eternal lens gives us patience and perseverance.
3. **Growing in Faith Over a Lifetime**
   Holiness and maturity do not happen overnight. They unfold over years of prayer, study, service, and refining through life's tests. We can be patient with ourselves and others, knowing God is committed to completing the good work He began in us (Philippians 1:6).
4. **Impact on Future Generations**
   The way we live our faith can set a standard for children, nieces, nephews, or younger friends. Even if we do not have children ourselves, others observe our life. A single act of kindness or consistent integrity can shape how they view God. Our influence can ripple across years.

---

7. Specific Areas to Keep Watching

1. **Emotional Health**
   Being spiritually healthy includes addressing emotional wounds. If you notice ongoing anxiety, depression, or unresolved trauma, consider reaching out to a counselor or wise church leader. Seeking help does not show weakness; it shows wisdom. Emotional healing can free us to grow stronger in Christ.
2. **Time Management**
   In a busy age, we might neglect spiritual duties or meaningful fellowship due to overload. Periodically review your schedule. Ask if certain activities drain you without bearing good fruit. With God's

guidance, prune what hinders you so you have enough room for devotion, rest, and serving in ways that matter.
3. **Financial Stewardship**
Money issues can create stress and tempt us to panic instead of trust. A good approach involves budgeting, avoiding debt when possible, giving generously, and seeking advice if needed. Handling finances responsibly can display faith and prevent worry from eating away at our peace.
4. **Moral Boundaries**
Traps like gossip, dishonesty, or impure entertainment can slip in if we are not watchful. Regularly evaluate your media intake, friendships, and personal habits. Where you see compromise, pray for strength to change. Maintaining clean moral boundaries protects your witness and keeps your heart aligned with God.

---

8. A Final Word on Hope and Perseverance

1. **Pressing Forward in Hope**
No matter how life evolves after reading this book, keep your hope intact. Hope is more than a dream; it is the anchor of your soul in God's steadfast promises. Some seasons will test that hope severely, but cling to it. Hope fuels perseverance, and perseverance leads to maturity.
2. **Celebrating Progress**
(Replacing the restricted word, we say "recognizing progress.") When you overcome a habit or lead someone to understand God's love, pause to acknowledge that milestone. This encourages you to press on. Give praise to God for the progress, remembering all good things come from His hand.
3. **Embracing Ongoing Learning**
Each chapter of this book touched on a specific area—like prayer, relationships, or trusting God with goals. But real life brings fresh problems daily. Stay teachable. Listen to new teachings, ask questions of mentors, and keep your heart open to learning. God will continue unveiling wisdom as you seek Him.
4. **Encouraging Each Other to Stand Firm**
We are not meant to walk alone. Keep strong bonds with friends

who share your faith. Check on each other's spiritual health, celebrate triumphs, and offer a hand in low points. Through mutual support, we grow more resilient and fruit-bearing in Christ.

9. A Blessing for the Future

1. **Prayer for God's Guidance**
   As you close this book, pray that God will show you the next steps He wants you to take. Whether it is developing a certain gift, reconciling a strained relationship, or starting a new spiritual practice, ask for clarity. Believe that He delights in guiding you when you seek Him wholeheartedly.
2. **Anticipation of Growth**
   Expect that you will continue to mature. Trials will come, but they can refine your faith. Joyful moments will also come, reminding you of God's goodness. Each experience, good or hard, can shape you more into the image of Christ if you keep your heart open to His work.
3. **Confidence in His Love**
   No matter what obstacles appear, hold fast to the truth that God's love for you is deep, personal, and unwavering. You never outgrow your need for that love, nor does God ever withdraw it. This truth remains a foundation when everything else shakes.
4. **Stepping Forward with Courage**
   Take the lessons, the scriptures, and the insights, and put them into action. Do not let them gather dust in your mind. If you feel afraid at any new challenge, recall that you serve an almighty God who calls you beloved. That knowledge can fuel your bravery in everyday acts of faith, kindness, and service.

10. Conclusion of Chapter 20

This book has aimed to encourage and equip you—wherever you stand in your walk of faith. From the earliest steps of learning about Jesus to deepening spiritual disciplines, from building healthy relationships to finding hope in hard seasons, each chapter addressed a key piece of a Christian woman's life. Now, as you reach the end, remember that this is really a beginning of another phase: applying these truths and continuing to learn beyond these pages.

Our God is a living God who interacts with us personally. He invites us to ongoing growth, offering fresh grace every morning. You can face tomorrow knowing that you do not do so alone. The Holy Spirit is with you, the Word of God is in your hands, and a community of believers stands ready to share the road. Keep your eyes on Christ, the pioneer and finisher of your faith, who promises to finish the good work He started in you.

In times of joy, thank Him wholeheartedly. In moments of sorrow, cling to Him for comfort. In confusion, seek His Word and wise counsel. In service, offer your gifts freely, trusting Him to multiply your efforts. Above all, rest in the knowledge that you are dearly loved, and no circumstance can break that bond. May God bless you as you walk forward, step by step, in faith, love, and the lasting hope found in Jesus Christ.

www.ingramcontent.com/pod-product-compliance
Lightning Source LLC
LaVergne TN
LVHW012043070526
838202LV00056B/5582